Cambridge Elements

Elements in Epistemology
Stephen Hetherington
University of New South Wales, Sydney

THE INDISPENSABILITY OF INTUITIONS

Marc A. Moffett
The University of Texas, El Paso

Shaftesbury Road, Cambridge CB2 8EA, United Kingdom

One Liberty Plaza, 20th Floor, New York, NY 10006, USA

477 Williamstown Road, Port Melbourne, VIC 3207, Australia

314–321, 3rd Floor, Plot 3, Splendor Forum, Jasola District Centre, New Delhi – 110025, India

103 Penang Road, #05–06/07, Visioncrest Commercial, Singapore 238467

Cambridge University Press is part of Cambridge University Press & Assessment, a department of the University of Cambridge.

We share the University's mission to contribute to society through the pursuit of education, learning and research at the highest international levels of excellence.

www.cambridge.org
Information on this title: www.cambridge.org/9781009544412

DOI: 10.1017/9781009544450

© Marc A. Moffett 2025

This publication is in copyright. Subject to statutory exception and to the provisions of relevant collective licensing agreements, no reproduction of any part may take place without the written permission of Cambridge University Press & Assessment.

When citing this work, please include a reference to the DOI 10.1017/9781009544450

First published 2025

A catalogue record for this publication is available from the British Library

ISBN 978-1-009-54441-2 Hardback
ISBN 978-1-009-54446-7 Paperback
ISSN 2398-0567 (online)
ISSN 2514-3832 (print)

Cambridge University Press & Assessment has no responsibility for the persistence or accuracy of URLs for external or third-party internet websites referred to in this publication and does not guarantee that any content on such websites is, or will remain, accurate or appropriate.

For EU product safety concerns, contact us at Calle de José Abascal, 56, 1°, 28003 Madrid, Spain, or email eugpsr@cambridge.org

The Indispensability of Intuitions

Elements in Epistemology

DOI: 10.1017/9781009544450
First published online: October 2025

Marc A. Moffett
The University of Texas, El Paso
Author for correspondence: Marc A. Moffett, mamoffett@utep.edu

Abstract: The idea that human beings possess a substantive source of non-experiential evidence (intuitions) has been ridiculed as mystical or hopelessly mysterious. This Element argues that intuitions are neither. On the contrary, it argues that intuitions are a ubiquitous and familiar feature of our cognitive lives and that their evidential status is no more puzzling than that of any other source of evidence. The author does not, however, parry this accusation by assimilating intuitions to less metaphysically uncomfortable entities. Assimilation is futile. Rather, they treat intuitions as their own kind of *sui generis* intentional states. But unlike many treatments of intuition, the focus is not on their role in the "a priori" disciplines. Instead, the author argues that eschewing intuitions undermines our knowledge on a very broad scale; they are epistemically indispensable. This Element constitutes a sustained argument for this conclusion.

Keywords: intuition, foundationalism, concept application, perception, inference

© Marc A. Moffett 2025

ISBNs: 9781009544412 (HB), 9781009544467 (PB), 9781009544450 (OC)
ISSNs: 2398-0567 (online), 2514-3832 (print)

Contents

1 Introduction   1
2 Moderate Dogmatism & Phenomenology   2
3 Non-Phenomenal Presentational Dogmatism   17
4 Intuition and Concept Application   31

    References   55

1 Introduction

The idea that human beings possess a substantive source of non-perceptual, non-introspective evidence has often been ridiculed as mystical or, at the very least, hopelessly mysterious. In this Element, I will argue that rational intuitions (hereafter, just intuitions) are neither. On the contrary, I will argue that intuitions are a ubiquitous and familiar feature of our cognitive lives and that their evidential status is no more or less puzzling than that of any other source of basic evidence. I will not, however, try to parry this accusation by assimilating intuitions to less metaphysically uncomfortable entities – beliefs of unclear epistemic basis, for instance, or inclinations to believe (Devitt 2006, 491; Gopnik and Schwitzgebel 1998; Kornblith 1998; Sosa 1996; Williamson 2007). Assimilation is futile.[1] In keeping with the rationalist tradition, I will treat intuitions as their own kind of *sui generis* intentional states. But unlike many treatments of intuition, my focus will not be on their role in the "*a priori*" disciplines. Indeed, for the most part, my focus will not be on the *a priori* at all. Instead, I will take a cue from Descartes and aim to establish that eschewing intuitions undermines our knowledge on a very broad scale; they are epistemically indispensable. This Element constitutes a single, sustained argument for this conclusion.

Consistent with many recent treatments, I will begin with the assumption that intuitions are a species of "seemings" which, along with introspective and perceptual experiences, serve as basic sources of evidence (moderate dogmatism). Unlike most recent treatments, however, I will not take the supposed "presentational phenomenology" of seemings or their contents to be their epistemically relevant feature. In Section 2, I develop a fully general argument against the epistemic significance of phenomenology by adapting Bealer's non-reductive functional definitions of the mental properties and relations to defend the possibility of phenomenal zombies. I then show that denying such creatures epistemic standing equivalent to our own would amount to a form of untenable, phenomenological chauvinism.

This argument motivates the development in Section 3 of a non-phenomenological theory of presentational states, which preserves moderate dogmatism by treating the epistemically significant feature of such states as involving a unique kind of cognitive *apprehension* of contents rather than a unique phenomenology. This non-phenomenological approach to seemings allows us to counter concerns like Williamson's "Absent Intuition Challenge" and counsels a different strategy for understanding intuitions – looking for their

---

[1] Bealer (1992), Huemer (2007), and Bengson (2015a), among others, offer persuasive considerations against various reductive theories of intuition.

cognitive and epistemic effects rather than looking directly for (phenomenally) conscious cognitive episodes. On this broadly Cartesian approach, intuitions serve to "fill in" the epistemic gap left unaccounted for by appeal to other sources of basic evidence (perceptual experience, introspection). So, when there is a mismatch between what seems justified (or, more generally, rationally non-aberrant) and what other sources of evidence can support, we have reason to suspect that intuitions come into play.

In Section 4, I make the case for the payoff of the non-phenomenological approach to intuitions, starting with a defense of the claim that they are essentially involved in concept application (as suggested by, e.g., Bealer 1992 and Strawson 1992). This allows for a natural understanding of how thought experiments (such as the Gettier cases) function that clearly distinguishes them from inferences (cf. Ludwig 2018, 390). Finally, I close by pressing their role in two important areas: inference and perception. Both inference and perception, I argue, essentially involve concept application and so intuition. If this is correct, it follows that all, or almost all, of our knowledge is intuition-dependent; that is, absent intuition, little or no knowledge (whether *a priori* or *a posteriori*) is possible, thereby yielding the central thesis of this Element – the indispensability of intuition.

2 Moderate Dogmatism & Phenomenology

2.1 Unified Foundationalism

Traditionally, perceptual experience, introspection, and intuition have figured prominently in foundationalist epistemology as sources of basic, regress-stopping evidence (reasons). And yet, on their face, these three kinds of cognitive state represent an exceptionally diverse array of cognitive capacities involving our access to the external world, our own mental world, and the conceptual world, respectively. Additionally, there seems to be little that they have in common with respect to their overall functional architecture or physical correlates. Given their purported epistemic commonality, this face-value diversity is puzzling. Is it mere happenstance that these states each serve as sources of basic evidence, with each state's epistemic significance being driven by idiosyncratic characteristics of that state? Or alternatively, is it possible that, despite their evident differences, all three states share some common feature or features that determine their epistemic similarities?

Unified Foundationalism maintains that the epistemic commonality between these states arises because they are all of a single cognitive type – they are all *seemings*.

- perceptual seemings
- introspective seemings
- conceptual seemings

According to this view, all three sources gain their epistemic significance in virtue of the fact that they are seemings, and not any idiosyncratic feature of the state. Unified Foundationalism thus promises to significantly simplify epistemic foundationalism by subsuming all sources of basic evidence under a unified framework.

While there are, in principle, many ways of carrying out this project, much recent epistemology has focused on some form of moderate dogmatism as the most promising approach (e.g., Huemer 2001; Pryor 2000):

Moderate Dogmatism (MD): If x has a seeming as of p's being the case, then x thereby has some degree of immediate (*prima facie*) propositional justification for believing that p.

As formulated here, MD is intended as a stand-in for a wide range of variously nuanced positions (including, in addition to Pryor and Huemer, Bengson 2015a, Chudnoff 2013, Moffett 2025, Schroeder 2021, and Tucker 2010, among many others).[2] So articulated, MD is consistent with both internalist and externalist epistemological theories. For example, Lyons' (2009) view is a form of reliabilist moderate dogmatism. However, for largely familiar reasons, I find epistemic externalism implausible (e.g., BonJour 1980, Cohen 1984). In my view, these traditional objections arise because, as Boghossian puts it, externalism fails "to connect with a thinker's responsibility for his cognitive practice" (2001, 634). As a result, externalist theories are unable to explain the underlying rationality of our cognitive actions (as opposed to mere cognitive processes). But, as I have argued elsewhere (Moffett 2025), it is the rationality of these cognitive actions that serves as the ultimate normative ground for our beliefs. It is this disconnect between cognitive action (specifically, judgment) and belief that ultimately undermines externalist epistemology.[3] For this reason, I will assume an internalist epistemological framework.

But while MD provides a pleasantly austere foundation for epistemology, it does little more than label the proposed common type as "seemings" and largely relies on our pre-philosophical grasp of seemings to account for what is epistemically significant about them. Consequently, an adequate theory of

---
[2] As far as I can tell, the views developed here are not at odds with theories like phenomenal explanationism (McCain & Moretti 2021) that subsume a dogmatist background.
[3] This point also animates the considerations about concept application (Section 4.1) and inferential acts (Section 4.3).

dogmatism needs to be fitted out with an account of why seemings are able to play the epistemic role attributed to them by MD.

2.2 Presentationality

The effort to spell out this epistemic project in detail has largely fallen to defenders of intuition whose focus has been to establish the epistemic *bona fides* of intuitions by showing that they possess the very properties that give perceptual seemings their epistemic significance (e.g., Bengson 2015a, Chudnoff 2013), a strategy Bengson dubs "quasi-perceptualism". Quasi-perceptualism makes sense. Whatever seemings are, perceptual experience had better be among them. Moreover, in pre-philosophical contexts, we already tend to analogize both introspection and intuition to the perceptual case.

For this reason, it will be useful to start by considering what seems to be epistemically significant about perceptual experience. And here, there is wide agreement that one of its most salient features is our sense that it *presents* or otherwise *reveals* reality.[4] Presentational states differ from "assertive representations" (like belief) in virtue of the fact that they present their contents as true or actual. The essential feature of such states is that they are *revelatory* in the sense that they are cognitive happenings that apparently reveal how things are. Tolhurst summarizes the idea thus: [S]eemings have the feel of truth, the feel of a state whose content reveals how things really are. Their felt givenness typically leads one to experience believing that things are as they seem as an objectively fitting or proper response to the seeming. When I merely think about there being a cat in my yard, imagine this to be the case, or desire that it be the case, my mental state does not have this feel. These states are not experienced as being revelatory of real features of the world. ... [S]eemings have the feel of being grounded in and revelatory of their objects, [so] we apprehend the formation of the corresponding belief to be epistemically proper or appropriate and hence take belief to be called for in response to these experiences" (1998, 298).

It is not implausible to think that the presentationality of perceptual experiences is the feature that confers on them their epistemic significance. After all, having "immediate consciousness of the existence of things outside of us", to use Strawson's (1979, 97) phrasing, is obviously relevant to forming beliefs concerning those things. Presentationality involves a kind of weak ontological connection to the world, though it falls short of a commitment to the world being the way it is presented. If so, then quasi-perceptualism would appear to recommend the following:

---

[4] Representative characterizations include (Bonjour 2004, 354; Broad 1952, 6; Levine 2006, 179; Strawson 1979, 97; Searle 1983, 45–46; Sturgeon 2000, 9).

Presentational Dogmatism (Presentationalism): If MD is true, this is in virtue of the fact that seemings are presentational states.[5]

Presentationalism captures the intuitive idea that it is *ceteris paribus* reasonable to accept that things are the way they are presented to us as being. But even granting its intuitive appeal, presentationalism still paints too broad a brush to yield a satisfactory theory seemings. Rather, it serves to focus our attention on what promises to be their key epistemic feature – the apparent "presentness" ("in-the-worldness", "actuality") of their contents.

However, most recent theorizing about presentationality has focused almost exclusively on what is arguably an incidental feature of presentational states as far as their epistemology is concerned, namely, their phenomenology. This preoccupation with phenomenology is perhaps an understandable side-effect of quasi-perceptualism. But importing the lens of perceptual phenomenology has done a disservice to the theory of intuitions, or so I will argue. Intuitions are not obviously experiential states, and we should be on guard against importing an experiential conceptual scheme into their characterization. And if intuitions don't share a phenomenology with experiences, then the unifying character of seemings must lie elsewhere. I will now argue that the key to presentationality lies not in "what-it's-like" for us, but rather in how we apprehend the information with which we are presented. This constitutes a fairly significant break, not only from most current theorizing about the epistemology of intuitions, but also from the epistemology of perception.

2.3 Against Phenomenalism

It has become philosophical orthodoxy that seemings *as a type* possess a distinctive phenomenology – presentational phenomenology – in virtue of which they have their epistemological import.

Phenomenal Presentational Dogmatism (Phenomenalism): Presentationality is or is grounded in (i) a distinctive phenomenological property, and (ii) it is in virtue of this property that seemings have the epistemic significance they have according to MD.

Huemer (2001) dubs his version of moderate foundationalism "*phenomenal conservatism*". Chudnoff (2013) is wholly concerned with "presentational

---

[5] Bengson (2024) aims to disentangle the theory of presentational states from the less clearly defined language of seemings. I am sympathetic to this suggestion, but since talk of seemings is so natural and so widespread in contemporary discussions, I will retain it. Nevertheless, it is intended here as a semi-technical notion and not an analysis of what Bealer calls the "indiscriminate use of the term".

phenomenology" and its epistemic significance. Bengson claims that presentationality "is a phenomenological property, concerning what it is like for a subject to be in such a state" (2024, 173). Smithies is explicit in claiming that "it is in virtue of the phenomenal character of its perceptually seeming to one that p that one has defeasible justification to believe that p" (2013, 737). Koksvik is similarly explicit: "[T]he claim isn't merely that intuition justifies belief and has a characteristic phenomenal character. The claim is that intuition justifies belief because it has that phenomenal character" (2021, 15).

Despite this consensus, there is good reason to be suspicious of Phenomenalism.[6] Let me begin by drawing a distinction between the phenomenology of presentational states and the conceptually distinct feature of apprehending something as present (actual, real, part of the world). For ease of reference, I will label the first property "presentational phenomenology" and the latter property "presentationality". It is a substantive philosophical question how presentational phenomenology and presentationality are related. The Phenomenalist asserts that presentationality is either reducible to or necessarily grounded in presentational phenomenology. Of course, some presentational states (perception, foremost among them) indisputably have a proprietary presentational phenomenology. And, indeed, we can grant for the sake of argument that all of them do, at least as a matter of fact. But it doesn't follow from this that presentational states possess their presentationality in virtue of their phenomenology, and so it doesn't follow that presentational states have their epistemic significance in virtue of that phenomenology (viz., Phenomenalism).

Prizing apart these two properties of seemings is difficult, and they are often run together in discussion. For example, Consider the following discussion of clairvoyance from Foster: "[I]n the clairvoyant cases, . . ., there is no provision for the presentational feel of phenomenal experience—for the subjective impression that an instance of the relevant type of environmental situation is directly presented" (2000, 112). Here, the appeal to the "presentational feel" of experience is clearly a reference to presentational phenomenology. But the case is under described: nothing in Foster's description entails that the "environmental situation" is not "directly presented". That result follows only if one tacitly identifies presentational phenomenology with presentationality. Because of this, it is natural to "fill in" the example in such a way that the clairvoyant

---

[6] Berger (2020) argues for a view that is in many ways similar to the one proposed here – though restricted to perceptual states. As will emerge, my argument is pitched at a more general level and, consequently, does not need to address questions of, e.g., unconscious perception. Related concerns may also be found in Ghijsen 2014; Berger, Nanay, & Quilty-Dunn 2018. Teng (2024) rejects Phenomenalism as stated but treats presentationality as a separate metacognitive feeling.

simply comes to (reliably) have otherwise inexplicable *beliefs* about the present environmental situation, absent any antecedent seeming (presentational state). And if that is how the story is understood, then we can agree that the clairvoyant's beliefs are unjustified (Bergmann 2006). But that doesn't show that it is presentational phenomenology, rather than presentationality, that is doing the epistemic work since both properties have been excised from the case. In order for such cases to support Phenomenalism over mere anti-Phenomenal Presentationalism, we would need to stipulate that the clairvoyant lacked any antecedent state with presentational phenomenology and yet possessed an antecedent state in which the situation was presented to her. This is, of course, akin to a state of "zombie perception" (Chalmers 1997) or super-blindsight (Block 1995).[7] And if we are attributing super-blindsight to the clairvoyant in Foster's example, my intuitions are that her beliefs are justified.[8] What matters is presentationality, not presentational phenomenology.

Smithies (2012, 2014, 2019) has argued that we should reject the considerations from super-blindsight just given. His argument is aimed at defending the following condition:

- *The Phenomenal Condition:* Necessarily, perception justifies beliefs about the external world if and only if it has some phenomenal character (2019, 77).[9]

In the Phenomenal Condition, Smithies deploys an anaphoric pronoun, "it", on the right-hand side of the biconditional. Taken at face value, the pronoun refers back to the perception relation on the left-hand side. So, we are supposed to be considering perception in the absence of phenomenology. How are we to understand the "unconscious" perceptual relation invoked here? In the context

---

[7] Blindsight is the ability of certain individuals suffering from cortical lesions (cortical blindness) to nevertheless respond to "unconscious" visual stimuli (Weiskrantz et al. 1974). Individuals suffering from blindsight report being blind in some part of their visual field (the blind field). Nevertheless, when presented with visual stimuli in the blind field and forced to guess about the nature of that stimulus, their guesses are more reliable than chance (among other capacities that suggest blindsight patients have some limited access to the information occurring in the blind field).

Block (1995, 246) distinguishes between super-blindsight and super-duper-blindsight, where the former provides "medium access" to information in the blind field while the latter provides "truly high-quality access". I will put aside the distinction between "grades of access" and treat super-blindsight as involving relatively high-quality access of the sort stipulated by Smithies in the discussion below.

[8] One caveat here. In Foster's case, the clairvoyant is blindfolded, and this raises the concern that her super-blindsight is involved in a kind of deviant causal chain that might undermine her justification. But this feature of the case is inessential.

[9] As stated, the Phenomenal Condition only requires having *some* phenomenal character and not presentational phenomenology. But merely having phenomenal character is not sufficient for immediate justification. So, the Phenomenal Condition is false as stated, even if a narrowed condition in terms of presentational phenomenology is available.

of the present discussion, there are two possibilities: (1) It possesses the property of presentationality (i.e., it is a presentational state), or (2) it does not possess this property (i.e., it is not a presentational state).[10]

In the first case, we have a paradigmatic case of super-blindsight. Below (Section 1.5), I will try to provide a positive characterization of such a state. If Presentationalism is true, it follows that such states provide justification for corresponding beliefs. And the anti-Phenomenalist will find intuitions about super-blindsight to support this conclusion. But the Phenomenalist must deny the cogency of case (1), since they take presentationality to be (or to be grounded in) presentational phenomenology. So, the Phenomenalist maintains that the situation must be as in case (2) – super-blindsight cannot be a presentational state. Of course, nobody is committed to the claim that non-presentational states provide immediate justification for beliefs, so the anti-Phenomenalist would agree. The challenge for the anti-Phenomenalist would be to explain why presentationality is absent, if (as she claims) it is not a phenomenological property. But the anti-Phenomenalist denies that case (2) is mandatory, and, consequently, rejects the challenge. So, we are at an impasse: To decide whether or not the Phenomenal Condition holds, we must *first* decide whether presentationality and presentational phenomenology can come apart. Cases like clairvoyance can only be adequately developed if we have already settled the disagreement and, consequently, cut no philosophical ice in this debate.

Smithies offers an argument that might appear to settle this impasse, but ultimately does not. We can agree that beliefs non-inferentially formed on the basis of *actual* blindsight are not justified. Smithies goes on to claim, however, "There is no relevant difference between super-blindsight and ordinary blindsight that could plausibly explain why justification is present in the first case, but absent in the second" (2019, 86). Here is his argument (Smithies 2021, 772; also 2019, 81):

(1) Blindsighted subjects are not disposed to form beliefs noninferentially about the blind field on the basis of unconscious visual information alone, but rather to withhold belief.
(2) Blindsighted subjects are not rationally defective in withholding belief.
(3) If they were failing to respond to justifying evidence provided by unconscious visual information, they would be rationally defective.
(4) Therefore, unconscious visual information in blindsight doesn't provide evidence that justifies beliefs about the blind field.

---

[10] The claim that blindsight cases involve *unconscious* visual stimuli is not uncontroversial (see, e.g., Phillips 2021; see Overgaard 2012 for an overview).

(5) The only relevant difference between blindsight patients and super-blindsighters is that the latter have an unprompted disposition to form beliefs based on unconscious visual information alone.[11]

(6) But merely adding an unprompted disposition to form beliefs about the blind field cannot be enough to justify beliefs that were not justified beforehand.

(7) Therefore, super-blindsighters' beliefs are not justified either.

This argument presupposes that what distinguishes ordinary blindsight from super-blindsight is nothing more than an unprompted disposition to form beliefs. But there is no reason for the anti-Phenomenalist to accept this.

The dispute we are currently considering is over the possibility of a blindsight state exhibiting presentationality. We can all agree to the stipulation that presentationality is not present in ordinary blindsight. But starting with a state that lacks presentationality and merely "dropping in" an unprompted disposition to believe on its basis does not commit the anti-Phenomenalist to accepting that the new state is presentational. So, the anti-Phenomenalist is free to diagnose Smithies' case as one in which presentationality is still absent, given that it is stipulated that there is no difference apart from the presence of the indicated disposition.

The same thing can be said of the other difference Smithies stipulates, namely, that "super-blindsight has the same ... degree of reliability and richness of [informational] content ... " as ordinary sight (2019, 85). If one thought that presentationality was a function of the content of a state, then it might be the case that adding in the full (non-phenomenological) informational content of perceptual states would commit the anti-Phenomenalist to accepting that such states are presentational. (I will argue in a moment that this is not what the anti-Phenomenalist should say.) But if they did do this, then the case Smithies describes is not one in which we have "merely added in a disposition to form beliefs." We have additionally changed the content from being non-presentational to being presentational.

Why think that the richness of content might matter to presentationality? The properties to which our sensory apparatus has access are not sufficient on their own to determine the robust perceptual experience of a voluminous, four-dimensional world. To achieve this robust content, our visual system engages in a variety of interpolation phenomena that are not present in blindsight (see, e.g., Aleci & Dutto 2024, 8; Celesia 2005). Absent such effects, it might be argued, our visual systems are surely not presentational or, at least, not

---

[11] Smithies: "[L]et's stipulate that the super-blindsighter forms beliefs about the blind field spontaneously ... " (p. 85).

presentational of a robust external world. On a content-based view of presentationality, however, one might think that including the full computational effects of the visual system might be sufficient for a kind of non-phenomenological form of presentationality. So, whether the anti-Phenomenalist thinks presentationality is content-based or not, Smithies' argument is inconclusive.[12]

Despite these considerations, I think the anti-Phenomenalist should opt for an attitude-based, rather than content-based, theory of presentationality. The argument for this stems from consideration of derealization disorder (Shorvon et al. 1946), which also cut against most forms of Phenomenalism. In derealization disorder, a person's perceptual experiences are intrinsically like our own. And yet the experiences are not taken as revelatory of a mind-independent world (Ferretti 2025). Just as blindsight offers an imperfect model of perceptual experience lacking phenomenology, derealization disorder offers an imperfect model of perception-like phenomenal states lacking presentationality (Miyazono 2021). Call these "derealization experiences".[13] In the limit, derealization experiences need not differ in their intrinsic phenomenology or informational content from ordinary perceptual experiences. So, derealization experiences are the mirror image of perfect hallucinatory experiences. In derealization cases, the experience is veridical, but non-presentational; in perfect hallucination, the experience is non-veridical but presentational. What derealization disorders show is that neither the informational content of nor the intrinsic phenomenology of perceptual states is sufficient for presentationality.[14]

Dokic and Martin (2017) suggest that the "sense of reality" missing in derealization disorder is an affective state, a metacognitive feeling that accompanies perception. But their discussion presupposes, rather than defends, a Phenomenalist metacognitive theory of presentationality: "[W]e use the phrase "sense of presence" in the most neutral way possible, as referring to some phenomenologically distinctive experience to the effect that perceived objects are present" (299).[15] Dokic and Martin's view pushes the Phenomenalist/anti-Phenomenalist debate to

---

[12] The main target of Smithies' argument is not the anti-Phenomenalist Presentationalist, but the anti-Presentationalist, specifically, the Reliablist. So, it is not surprising that his arguments won't neatly address the former position.

[13] Dokic and Martin (2017, 302) claim, "It is empirically plausible that they [i.e., derealization disorder patients] have genuine perceptual experiences of the world." Insofar as one intends to use "perceptual experiences" and "perceptual seemings" interchangeably, I do not think this is correct. However, if one wishes to use "perceptual experiences" to capture a broader class of sensory states that does not entail apprehending-as-actual, I have no objection. But such states cannot play the epistemic role required by MD.

[14] This line of argument leaves open the possibility of a hybrid attitudinal/content theory of presentationality. I am skeptical. On the view I develop in §2, nothing prevents minimal perceptual contents from being presented, but this is not an issue I will try to settle.

[15] Other approaches include Riccardi (2019) and Ferretti (2025).

a different point in cognition. And predictably, as far as I can tell, the same sorts of disagreements will arise. For this reason, I want to now turn to an argument that aims to settle this debate at the most general level.

2.4 Self-Consciousness and Zombie Cognition

Chalmers notes "many everyday mental concepts straddle the fence, having both a phenomenal and psychological [i.e., causal/functional] component. ... Our everyday concept of pain [for example] presumably combines the two in some subtle weighted combination, but for philosophical purposes things are clearer if we keep them separate" (1997, 17). How best to understand the phenomenon Chalmers is gesturing at is not obvious. One approach is bifurcationism: We have independent functional and phenomenal concepts of the psychological and phenomenal mentals, respectively (Smithies 2019, 12). Smithies argument against (this form of) bifurcationism is that once we accept that many phenomenal properties lack functional definitions, there is no principled reason to exclude these phenomenal properties in the functional definitions of the psychological properties. As a result, even the psychological properties will have phenomenally individuated definitions (Smithies 2012, 347 2019, 14).

I think Smithies' claim about the phenomenal individuation of the psychological properties is correct. However, I will argue that even so, we have good reason to reject Phenomenalism. Here is how I will proceed: First, I will argue that it is possible to give *non-reductive* definitions of a natural sequence of *determinable* mental properties, of which the *standard* mental properties (pain, belief, etc.) are determinates. Given this, I will argue that the non-phenomenal correlates of the standard *phenomenal* mentals are themselves determinants of these determinable properties. The claim is not that these functional correlates *are* the standard phenomenal mentals; it is merely to claim that they are natural (i.e., non-Cambridge) mental states. In other words, we can introduce phenomenal zombies directly at the level of the mental properties and states independently of considerations of physicalism. We might call these "Cartesian zombies".[16] The resulting view is that the functionally defined determinable mental properties that are not essentially phenomenal – some of their determinates are non-phenomenal. I will then argue for two claims: (i) that the beliefs of Cartesian zombies are epistemically evaluable, and (ii) that their beliefs are justified by moderate dogmatism, if ours are. Since Cartesian zombies lack

---

[16] Traditional zombies already have this feature insofar as it is (mistakenly) granted that the standard reductive functional definitions define mental states. In other words, the "Hard Problem" is a problem about locating phenomenology in a functional world, not locating phenomenology in a physical world. See also Flanagan & Polger (1995).

presentational phenomenology, the moderate dogmatist is forced to either abandon Presentationalism or develop a non-phenomenological theory of presentationality. In Section 3, I defend the latter response.

I begin with a brief exposition of the Self-Consciousness Argument against reductive functionalism (Bealer 1997, 2010). Recall the standard way of formulating Ramsified definitions of the mentals (Lewis 1970; Ramsey 1931).

(A_1) x believes that p *iff* $(\exists r_1, \ldots, r_n)(P<r_1, \ldots, r_n>$ & $x\ r_j$s that p)
(A_2) x is in pain *iff* $(\exists r_1, \ldots, r_n)(P<r_1, \ldots, r_n>$ & x is in r_i)
⋮

Where P is the realization formula for psychological theory, $\mathcal{P}$, and $r_1, \ldots, r_n$ are property variables, r_j is the realizer property corresponding to the "belief role", and r_i is the realizer property corresponding to the "pain role". Standardly, the range of the quantifiers in Ramsified definitions is restricted to first-order realizer properties. This yields the familiar second-order functional definitions. The Self-Consciousness Argument then proceeds as follows: First-order realizer states (and, specifically, neural correlates of the mentals) won't satisfy the standard reductive definitions because $\mathcal{P}$ will contain mental predicates in intensional contexts, such as the following Self-Intimation Principle:

$\mathcal{I}$: If x believes that p and is engaged in introspection, x will <u>believe</u> that x <u>believes</u> that p.[17]

If clauses like $\mathcal{I}$ are included in $\mathcal{P}$, as they should be, and the quantifiers are restricted to first-order realizer states, we either get the intentional contents wrong (e.g., our beliefs are about the first-order realizer state rather than the mental state itself, call this the "wrong content objection") or we leave the embedded mental properties unreduced on the right hand side. Either way, the reductive definitions fail because mental relations exhibit a characteristic intensional, non-well-foundedness that they can't adequately capture.[18]

---

[17] An anonymous reviewer objects that I am here and elsewhere making claims about the nature of psychological states "from the armchair" when these are empirical claims that cannot be settled by introspective reflection alone. However, this discussion is largely neutral between analytic functionalism and psychofunctionalism (see Block 1980 for this distinction). It is true that in giving principles like $\mathcal{I}$, I am placing "armchair" constraints of a very general sort on psychological theorizing, namely, that it must capture the intensional non-well-foundedness of the mentals. $\mathcal{I}$ is a stand-in for whatever specific principles psychology ultimately settles on to capture our introspectively obvious capacity to think about our own mental states, including our own beliefs. It is implausible that psychological theorizing floats wholly free from such evident "armchair" considerations. Indeed, as I have argued elsewhere (Moffett 2010), it will be necessary to place considerably stronger armchair constraints on psychofunctional definitions if they are to avoid inappropriate forms of psychological chauvinism.

[18] For critical discussion, see McCullagh (2000) and Tooley (2001), and Bealer (2000, 2001) for replies. Båve (2017) is an attempt to avoid the argument using conceptual role semantics for LOT

But the failure of the standard reductive functional definitions points the way to *non-reductive* functional definitions. In non-reductive definitions, the quantifiers are *not* restricted to first-order realizer properties but are allowed to range over the referents of the theoretical vocabulary itself.[19] The standard mentals will thus trivially satisfy the non-reductive formulas. Assuming that intensional non-well-foundedness (hereafter, just non-well-foundedness) is unique to the standard mental properties and relations, *only* the standard mentals will satisfy them, at least when they are restricted in certain ways to rule out various non-natural properties (see Bealer 2010, 155). This uniqueness assumption yields the kind of non-reductive functional definitions defended by Bealer.

Unfortunately, Bealer's version of non-reductive functionalism appears unable to account for the intuitive possibility of non-standard, but also non-Cambridge, alternative realizers. For instance, it is intuitively possible for there to be a being that satisfies the non-reductive definitions but whose "pain role" state differs phenomenologically from our own. Such a being might have a "pain-role state" with a familiar quale, such as the quale we associate with nausea (e.g., Lewis 1983) or with an alien quale with which we are unfamiliar. On the plausible assumption that pain has its quale essentially, these phenomenologically distinct, but functionally equivalent, states will not count as pains.[20] Call these sequences the "alien mentals". Consequently, the non-reductive definitions as originally developed by Bealer will not uniquely isolate the standard mentals.[21]

Nevertheless, the non-reductive definitions can still be understood as defining a sequence of *determinable* properties of which both the standard mentals and the alien mentals will be *determinates*.[22] Consider again the Self-Intimation Principle above:

$\mathcal{G}$: If x believes that p and is engaged in introspection, x will believe that x believes that p.

Ramsifying, we get:

I: $(\exists r_1, r_2, r_3)$(If x r_1 that p and is engaged in r_2, x will r_1 that x r_1 that p)

---

sentences. As I read him, he does this by effectively denying the *intensional* non-well-foundedness of the mentals and concedes that if this is not done, the argument goes through. Given the relative immediacy of our access to our own mental states, I find this response implausible.

[19] See Wilson (1999) and Shoemaker (2001) for a different development of non-reductivism.

[20] For discussion of the complexity of our pain concept, see (Borg et. al. 2020, Liu 2023)

[21] Thanks to Chad Carmichael for extended discussion on this point. If you think that the mentals don't have their qualia essentially, then Bealer's original definitions will go through. But in that case, the remainder of my argument can proceed unchanged.

[22] I am here adopting the terminology of determinate/determinable from Yablo (1992). However, it may be that the relation invoked here and by Yablo is not that of determination (see Funkhouser 2023). As far as I can tell, nothing turns on this, and the simplicity of the vocabulary makes it useful to express the point this way.

If we uniformly substitute the standard mentals into this formula, we get back 𝒢 and thereby avoid the wrong-content objection. On the other hand, if we substitute in the alien mentals, we get back 𝒢*.

> 𝒢*: If x a-believes that p and is engaged in a-introspection, x will a-<u>believe</u> that x a-<u>believes</u> that p.

When we Ramsify over the intensional content, we remove what was specific to that content and only retain the pattern of non-well-founded embedding. As we saw, this is what generates the wrong content objection for the physicalist. But the non-reductive definitions yield the correct content for our non-well-founded beliefs; they are about the standard mentals themselves and not their physical correlates. Similarly, as we can see from 𝒢*, alien beliefs will be about the alien mentals. So, the Ramsified formulas, when not type-restricted to physical realizer states as they are in reductive functionalism, don't falter on the wrong content objection.

We achieve this result by changing how the Ramsified formulas are derived. We start with *the characteristic pattern of one of the determinate (realizer) property sequences rather than the characteristic pattern of the properties to be defined.* We can do this because no effort is being made to provide an ontological reduction of the mental realizer properties, which is an independent desideratum of traditional functionalism. The result is a definition of the functional mental type (by a form of abstraction from its instances) under which the standard mental properties and relations are subsumed.

> (A′$_1$) x determinably believes that p *iff* ($\exists r_1, \ldots, r_n$)(P<$r_1, \ldots, r_n$> & x r_js that p)
> (A′$_2$) x is in determinable pain *iff* ($\exists r_1, \ldots, r_n$)(P<$r_1, \ldots, r_n$> & x is in r_i)
> $\vdots$

In words: x determinably believes that p if and only if there exists some sequence of properties that satisfies core psychology and x is in the state that corresponds to the belief role in that sequence. Unlike Bealer's non-reductive functional definitions, these definitions are typed (i.e., the variables should be understood as being restricted to realizer states). If the determinable sequence was required to satisfy the pattern as well, we would end up back in the grips of the self-consciousness argument. This is because the determinables of the non-well-founded states would then be non-well-founded and so would have the determinable states as their contents, as follows:

> 𝒢**: If x determinably believes that p and is engaged in determinable introspection, x will *determinably* believe that x *determinably* believes that p.

But there is no reason to suppose that the determinable properties satisfy a determinable-level self-intimation principle. When I believe that I have beliefs, I do not *also* determinably believe that I have determinable beliefs!

Assuming that the standard mentals have their core functional roles essentially, we can now give hybrid functional definitions of them as follows:

(A″$_1$) x believes that p *iff* (∃r$_1$, …, r$_n$)(P<r$_1$, …, r$_n$> & x r$_j$s that p & r$_j$ is Φ)
(A″$_2$) x is in pain *iff* (∃r$_1$, …, r$_n$)(P<r$_1$, …, r$_n$> & x is in r$_i$ & in r$_i$ is Ψ)
⋮

Where Φ and Ψ are whatever additional properties distinguish determinate belief and determinate pain. In the case of pain, for instance, Ψ will include the phenomenological features of pain. Let us symbolize this by P-PAIN. But the definitions of the determinate states need not be as simplistic as "satisfies the pain role and has P-PAIN". For instance, it is plausible that pain satisfies the "pain role" (in conjunction with the other members of its sequence) *in virtue of* possessing the phenomenology, P-PAIN, that it possesses. Such a view would make the phenomenology of pain a way of satisfying the "pain role" isolated by the determinable:

(A‴$_2$) x is in pain *iff* (∃r$_1$, …, r$_n$)(P<r$_1$, …, r$_n$> & x is in r$_i$ & r$_i$ satisfies P in virtue of having P-PAIN)

But satisfying P in virtue of having pain phenomenology is only one way of coming to satisfy P. Alien pain phenomenology is another.

But once we accept that there are multiple ways for mental states to satisfy the "pain role", it is difficult to resist the otherwise intuitive conclusion that some of them are purely informational (non-phenomenological) ways of doing so. The "pain role", after all, is an informationally defined role. So long as there is even a logical possibility of access to the relevant information without p-consciousness, we will have to concede that there are p-unconscious states that can play the pain role and, so, not all determinates of determinable-pain are phenomenological states.[23]

What goes for pain, however, also goes for presentational states. Koksvik (2017, 17) claims that "the centrality of [the phenomenology of intuitions] to the nature

---

[23] Are these alternative sequences genuinely mental sequences? Yes. By hypothesis, zombies have "cognitive states" that are functionally comparable to our own insofar as they satisfy P. As Fodor (1974; Oppenheim & Putnam 1958) contends, owing to our psychological complexity, the psychological properties and principles governing our cognitive lives will be emergent in that there will be no non-disjunctive reduction from the psychological level to any lower scientific level (for a recent survey see Robertson & Wilson 2024). But then satisfaction of P would plausibly be sufficient for a sequence to count as a mental sequence, since it will fall at the same ontic or explanatory level as the "standard mentals".

and epistemology questions can be approached separately. In practice, this is not really the case." But the preceding argument shows that this is wrong. We can concede to the Phenomenalist, even if just for the sake of argument (see Section 2.2 below), that all of our presentational states satisfy their psychological and epistemic roles (at least in part) in virtue of their distinctive phenomenology. But this does not imply that all of the determinants of the (determinable) presentational states possess this phenomenology. Consequently, we can consider the epistemic standing of presentational states independently of questions about phenomenology.

Given this, the Phenomenalist is faced with a dilemma. We are assuming foundationalism and, specifically, moderate dogmatism. I will further assume that such fundamental epistemic principles are not merely contingent, but necessary. Now, we have granted to the Phenomenalist that our seeming states are intrinsically phenomenological and even that they have a proprietary presentational phenomenology. According to Phenomenalism, our foundational beliefs are justified in virtue of this presentational phenomenology. But what does the Phenomenalist say about the beliefs of our non-phenomenological (zombie) counterparts? Either she must assert that, despite the psychological and functional overlap with us, our zombie counterparts are not capable of having justified beliefs, or she must assert that our zombie counterparts' foundational beliefs are justified differently than ours.

Accepting the first horn of this dilemma is implausible once it is conceded that our zombie counterparts are fully minded beings whose cognition and behavior are governed by the same core set of psychological principles as our own. The intuition here is that the very substantive psychological similarity between us and zombies is sufficient to establish their epistemic evaluability. This is not merely because of their functional overlaps, but because their psychology results in what is substantially the same view of the world as the one we have by way of the same basic psychological processes.

In fact, because $\mathcal{P}$ captures the core psychological laws governing our cognition, it is arguable that the addition of phenomenological states adds nothing of significance. Notice, for instance, that if we apply Yablo's (1992) proportionality test for mental causation, we get the result that it is the determinable property (rather than any phenomenal determinate) that is proportionate to the effect. Levy notes that "there is nothing that we can do that [zombies] can't. . . . They are able to exercise control over their actions. Indeed, they seem capable of fulfilling almost any proposed sufficient conditions of moral [and, we might add, epistemic] responsibility" (2014, 28). And, indeed, while it is true that zombies lack phenomenal consciousness, this does not imply that their cognitive lives collapse into mere subpersonal informational states or that they lack agency. Neither does lacking p-consciousness imply that zombies do not occupy a point of view or occupy the center of an "arena of presence" (Johnston 2007).[24] Such ideas will need recasting in terms of *de se* attitudes (in the first case) or non-phenomenological awareness, such as access consciousness (in the second case). But recovering the purely functional correlates of such states does not seem to be impossible in principle. Moreover, while I personally do not think we should identify consciousness with phenomenal consciousness, settling this debate is not necessary. If zombie minds are not conscious in any sense, so much the worse for the normative significance of (p-)consciousness. Though heterodox, this is not a new claim. Some philosophers have argued independently that consciousness plays no essential epistemic role whatsoever (esp. Berger 2020; see also Berger et al. 2018; Jenkin, 2020; Siegel, 2017). So, we have good reason to accept that zombies can have justified beliefs. However, if the Phenomenalist is right about foundational justification, the zombies' foundational beliefs are not justified and, in consequence, none of their beliefs are justified. This pushes the Phenomenalist to the second horn of the dilemma.

But accepting the second horn is self-undermining for the Phenomenalist. We share the same functional cognitive architecture as zombies. Consequently, any acceptable theory of foundational justification for zombies based on that architecture should be equally applicable to us. For instance, if the foundational beliefs of zombies are justified by way of reliabilism, then so should ours be. But if so, then in the interest of philosophical generality, this alternative account of foundational justification should be preferred, rendering the Phenomenalist account superfluous.

I conclude that the defender of Presentationalism should abandon Phenomenalism and seek a non-phenomenological theory of presentationality. In the next section, I will develop such a theory and provide additional motivation for it.

3 Non-Phenomenal Presentational Dogmatism

3.1 Seemings as a Posture of Cognition

I will begin by simply stating the theory of presentationality I favor. Call this the Attitudinal Theory of Presentationality (ATP).

> An intentional state, ψ, with content, C, is presentational *iff* ψ-ing is a cognitive happening in which C is apprehended-as-actual.

The idea is that apprehending-as-actual is a primitive, involuntary mode of grasping certain contents, a mode in which those contents are related to as being

---

[24] Thanks to John Bengson for discussion on this point.

actual (existent, instantiated, or otherwise "in the world"). Presentationality so understood is something like the non-phenomenal correlate of what philosophers often refer to as the "phenomenal force" of seemings. Kriegel, in characterizing the Brentanian take on ontological commitment, characterizes a similar attitude as follows: "[T]o think that Obama exists is to represent-as-existent Obama. The content of the thought is thus exhausted by Obama. Existence does not come into the thought at the level of content, but at the level of attitude" (Kriegel 2015, 87). This manner of grasping is distinct from the mode of apprehension associated with assertive states like belief, in which we accept *that* Obama exists. Stout characterizes such attitudinal differences as involving different "postures of consciousness" (Stout 2013 (1896), 40). But since "consciousness" now is so frequently taken to mean phenomenal consciousness, it will be better to call them different "postures of cognition". Clearly, we can assertively apprehend that Obama exists. But this apprehension is distinct from the kind of non-propositional apprehension Kriegel is characterizing, which we could characterize as apprehending-as-existent Obama.

I am drawing a different distinction between two different postures of cognition than the ones with which Brentano and Kriegel are concerned. Both presentational cognitions (seemings) and beliefs (or judgments) ostensibly connect us to (some part of) the world, but they do so in different ways. The difference does not – or at least need not – be a matter of differences in their contents. Even if seemings, like judgments and beliefs, have propositional contents, the relations differ in two crucial respects. First, beliefs are commitments while seemings are not. If someone believes that p, they are committed to the truth of p; but if it seems to them that p, they need not accept that p and, indeed, may reject it.[25] Second, the states differ in their agential status.[26] Judgments are cognitive actions and beliefs result from such actions; seemings, however, are occurrences. This difference is essential to the presentationality of seemings – nothing which is in our voluntary control (or which directly results from the exercise of such control) could plausibly be revelatory in the way seemings are.

On ATP, presentationality is about the *manner* in which contents are apprehended and not about what it is like to apprehend those contents in that manner. Presentational states differ from "assertive" states (like belief) in much the way assertive states differ from merely contentful states (like considering). There is no reason to treat these differences in cognitive posture or our knowledge of

---

[25] Similarly, even if we suppose that seemings have non-propositional contents, they differ from objectual belief-like commitments such as believing-in (see Textor 2021, 7–9).

[26] "Judging is always a doing as opposed to an undergoing, I.e., as opposed to the passive attitude we meet with, in say, feeling–: but in presentation too, strictly speaking" (Meinong 1983 (1902), 243).

them as inherently phenomenological. To co-opt an Anscombean idea about our knowledge of actions, I generally "know without observation" that I believe that p or that I am considering that p (Anscombe 1957). Even if these states, in fact, have an associated cognitive phenomenology, my introspective awareness of them is not mediated by that phenomenology (e.g., Gertler 2011). Kirk Ludwig makes a similar point, saying that even if intuitions have a distinctive phenomenology, "neither it nor the recognition of it is what warrants or justifies the proposition judged" (2007, 136–137; see also his 2010).[27]

It will be useful in what follows to have a simple way of representing these different postures of cognition without having to write out the full characterization each time. To that end, I will deliberately psychologize Frege's content and judgment/assertion operators and introduce a new one for presentational attitudes:

a. – that p (e.g., considering, entertaining)
b. ⊢ that p (e.g., believing)
c. ⊣ that p (e.g., seeming)

In (a)-(c), the operators are not intended to modify the content of the 'that'-clause, but to characterize the "posture" of the attitude taken toward that content.

Such states allow us to formulate a non-phenomenological version of presentational dogmatism that can generalize across all of the epistemic subjects we considered above:

Non-Phenomenal (Presentational) Dogmatism (ND): Presentationality is (i) the occurrence of an intentional relation whose posture is that of apprehending-as-actual its contents, and (ii) it is in virtue of this apprehension that seemings have the epistemic significance attributed to them by MD.

ND does not presuppose that presentational states lack an intrinsic phenomenology. As noted in Section 2.4, accepting ND does not even involve denying that some (or all) of our presentational states are presentational in virtue of their phenomenology. Nor does it presuppose that presentationality in us lacks an associated cognitive phenomenology. It merely asserts that in presentational states, it is the nature of the apprehension (and not their phenomenology, if any) that underpins the epistemic significance of seemings.[28]

---

[27] Ludwig's positive account of the epistemology of intuitions in terms of etiology differs from the one presented here, though we agree that intuition is centrally connected to concept possession and application (2007, 137).

[28] As an anonymous referee has remarked, ND provides a direct response to Moon's (2012) argument that seemings cannot provide doxastic justification for stored beliefs. Here is his argument:

3.2 Presentational Phenomenology: Some Problem Cases

I noted above that one danger of quasi-perceptualism is that we risk coercing other types of seemings into this same mold by including epistemically inessential features of perception. The goal of Section 2 was to call into question the epistemic importance of phenomenology, an importance that seems almost inevitable when perception is our primary model. In Section 3.1, I offered a positive characterization of presentationality that was phenomenologically neutral, allowing non-phenomenological or weakly phenomenological states to count as presentational even though they fail to have a "presentational phenomenology". But to this point, I have been neutral on the question of whether any of our seemings lack presentational phenomenology. Having opened up the conceptual space for a non-phenomenological approach, it is to this that I now turn.

In this subsection, I will canvass some problem cases that put pressure on the idea that presentational phenomenology is significant for a range of our own presentational states, including intuition. The goal is to provide some initial motivation for ATP by reconsidering these cases in light of the preceding discussion. In the next subsection, I will consider the case of intuition in detail.

The Absent State Objection

Many serious-minded philosophers follow Williamson and altogether deny having any phenomenological awareness of intuitions: "For myself, I am aware of no intellectual seeming beyond my conscious inclination to believe the Gettier proposition. Similarly, I am aware of no intellectual seeming beyond my conscious inclination to believe Naïve Comprehension, which I resist because I know better" (2007, 217).

Sosa suggests "that nothing like sensory experience seems to mediate analogously between facts known intuitively and beliefs through which they are known. ... [N]o sensory experiences mediate between fact and belief, nor does anything *like* sensory experience play that role" (2006, 208–209). Tucker explains the problems as follows: "I understand what a belief is.

---

(1) Tim knows that the law of non-contradiction is true (LN) while he naps (Premise)
(2) Tim does not believe LN on the basis of any evidence while he naps (Premise)
(3) Tim knows LN while he naps, and he does not believe LN on the basis of any evidence while he naps.

According to Moon (2) it is true because "[i]t seems impossible that the event of its seeming to you that LN, or any other seeming, could occur while you dream" (2012, 314). Moon's intuition here seems to be that seemings are phenomenological states and such states exist only when occurrent. But ND denies the phenomenological claim in favor of an attitudinal claim. And there is no obstacle to seemings serving as an evidential basis for dispositional beliefs (for a defense of the basing claim for stored seemings, see McCain & Stapleford 2024).

I understand what an inclination to believe is. When I introspect, I can find beliefs and inclinations to believe. But I don't have a grip on some *sui generis* propositional attitude thing you call a "seeming," and I can't find it when I introspect" (2013, 5). The thinness of intuitional phenomenology is hardly controversial. Bengson, for instance, concedes that "intuition tends to lack the rich sensory phenomenology of most perceptual experience" (2015a, 715). And Chudnoff concedes that the phenomenology of intuition is "elusive, difficult to describe, and partial" (2011, 643).

Williamson and others take these introspective considerations a step further in order to call into question the existence of intuitions as distinct pre-doxastic states that play the role proposed by MD. Instead, they assimilate them to cognitive states we can readily locate in introspection, such as inclinations to believe. This eliminativist/reductivist conclusion is understandable given Phenomenalism and quasi-perceptualism. Phenomenologically, no cognitive event remotely analogous to a perceptual presentational phenomenology seems to antecede our intuitive judgments. Since such phenomenology is so widely taken to define presentational states, it is hardly surprising that skeptics will draw the conclusion that there are no such antecedent intuitions.

The Absent (Weak) Phenomenology Objection

Even when we look at other perceptual modalities, we should be suspicious of a heavy reliance on phenomenology. Anscombe (1957) famously introduced the class of "things we can know without observation" by appeal to our knowledge of the position of our limbs. She claims. "If only my leg had been bent, there would very likely have been just that fact and my knowledge of it, that is, my capacity to describe my position straight off: no question of any appearance of the position to me, of any sensations which give me the position" (1981, 73). Huemer makes a similar claim: "It is possible to have perceptual experiences that lack qualia. . . . . The only actual example I can think of is awareness of the position of one's body (proprioception). . . . This is a sense over and above the five senses, although most people are unaware of it . . . . The reason they are not aware of it is that proprioception has no qualia. It represents one's body as being positioned in a certain way, but there is no special feeling or other "what-it's-like" to it – the only noticeable manifestation of proprioceptive "experiences" is that one is inclined to think one's body is positioned a certain way" (2001, 67). What Huemer says here precisely mirrors Williamson's claims about intuition. However, neither Anscombe nor Huemer suggests that there is no antecedent state they merely deny any phenomenologically salient antecedent state. The crucial point, however, is that the "phenomenology of proprioception" (if any) is sufficiently thin that careful thinkers can find it difficult to locate cognitively, thereby calling into question how much epistemic work it can bear. By contrast, ATP can easily account for Anscombe's and Huemer's reports.

The Wrong Phenomenology Objection

Moore claims that "the moment we try to fix our attention upon consciousness and to see what, distinctly, it is, it seems to vanish: it seems as if we had before us a mere emptiness. When we try to introspect the sensation of blue, all we can see is the blue: the other element is as if it were diaphanous.... [T]hat which makes the sensation of blue a mental fact seems to escape us; it seems, if I may use a metaphor, to be transparent – we look through it and see nothing but the blue" (1903, 450). Moore's observation causes problems for Phenomenalism. It is clear that I can introspectively determine that I am having a visual experience despite the lack of phenomenology of those states – what Moore describes as a "mere emptiness". But because this introspective awareness is phenomenologically transparent, its phenomenology, and in particular its presentational phenomenology, is the phenomenology of the visual experience itself (that is, the content of the visual experience and not the content of the introspective state). Speaks puts the point thus: "[The] idea is that introspection reveals nothing which is not an aspect of how the scene before one is presented as being; we notice only the objects that are represented as being in one's environment, and the properties those objects are represented as having. I think (un-originally) that this claim is phenomenologically plausible..." (2009, 541–542). It is unclear that introspecting visual experiences involves its own distinctive phenomenology, much less a distinctive presentational phenomenology.

ATP does not face this objection since it doesn't require any introspective phenomenology for presentational states. Instead, if I am having a visual appearance as of φ, this view merely asserts that I (introspectively) apprehend-as-actual my visual appearance (though not its content). In fact, since I apprehend-as-actual my visual appearance and my visual appearance has phenomenal character Φ, ATP predicts that when I introspect φ, Φ will occur as part of the content of my introspection. That is, it predicts the transparency of perceptual seemings.[29] There is much more to be said about introspection on the

---

[29] Apprehending-as-actual is not transitive in this way, however. If I perceptually apprehend (-as-actual) that p and I introspectively apprehend that I perceptually apprehend that p, it doesn't follow that I introspectively apprehend that p. This would be to commit a fallacy of decomposition.

It is also perhaps worth observing that if intuitions had a phenomenology, ATP predicts that it too will be transparent to intuition for the reason just given. So, one way of thinking about the Absent State Challenge is that when we introspect our intuitions, our *introspective* states lack any associated intellectual presentational phenomenology. Identifying presentationality with a type

proposed theory, but it is beyond the scope of this Element. The narrow point here is that the widely accepted transparency of introspective seemings vis-à-vis visual experiences supports skepticism about the significance of phenomenology for MD, and thereby, provides some prima facie motivation for ND.

Each of the cases just considered poses a *prima facie* difficulty for Phenomenalism by providing a scenario where presentationality is supposed to be doing significant epistemic work, but it can't because either there is no (adequate) phenomenology or because it is the wrong phenomenology. It is also striking how widespread these problems are, spanning intuition, introspection, and some perceptual modalities. Moreover, looking at other sensory modalities (olfaction, audition, and the sense of touch), it isn't obvious that they display the kind of robust *presentational* phenomenology of visual experience. This makes it look like the strategy of quasi-perceptualism may have selected the outlier case, thereby distorting not just the general theory of presentationality but our account of those non-visual states themselves.

I do not have the space to address possible Phenomenalist responses to all these cases. Instead, I will consider Williamson's Absent Intuition Challenge, since intuition is the primary focus of this Element. This will also be useful since I will use Williamson's challenge as a foil in developing the argument for the ubiquity and indispensability of intuitions in Section 4.

3.3 The Absent Intuition Challenge in Detail

Williamson's challenge constitutes an especially important challenge to Phenomenalism. The problem it poses is that, according to Phenomenalism, intuitions need to not only have a phenomenology, but a very specific and, arguably, cognitively salient phenomenology in virtue of which they justify (propositionally, and ultimately, doxastically) corresponding beliefs. In a case like Williamson's, therefore, the Phenomenalist must provide a plausible account of two things: (1) how he (and, of course, others) can have such a phenomenology and yet be so flatly unaware of it; and (2) how despite his apparent lack of awareness of this purportedly essential phenomenology, his intuitive beliefs can, nevertheless, be appropriately based on it to yield doxastic justification.[30] This puts considerable pressure on Phenomenalism as a theory of presentationality (and, no doubt, Presentationalism in general). If there are

---

of phenomenology, Williamson reasonably concludes that there are no intellectual seemings unless they are doxastic inclinations or judgments (which are phenomenologically present).

[30] Williamson, of course, is merely a useful stand-in for anyone who would infer from the widely accepted "thinness" of intuitional phenomenology (as noted in the previous subsection) to the denial of intuitions as distinct from more phenomenologically salient states, like inclinations to believe.

seemings that lack the robust phenomenology of visual experience or otherwise deviate from it, this will imply that Phenomenalists are placing a great deal of foundational weight on a very thin or eccentric phenomenological base. How might the Phenomenalist respond?

In response to Williamson's challenge, Chudnoff writes, "The most satisfying response is to insist that Williamson and other doxasticists do sometimes have intuition experiences, and to diagnose and repair their inability to *find* them" (2011, 644). According to Chudnoff, intuitions are *sui generis* states, but they are constituted by other "co-located" phenomenological states – thoughts, imaginings, intentions beliefs, etc. – organized according to some unifying principle. According to this view, because doxasticists are looking for a distinct, isolated state, they fail to find the intuition which is "co-located" with these other phenomenological states. As an analogy, this would be like failing to see a celestial constellation because you can only perceptually "find" the individual stars that constitute it.

But Chudnoff's response is unpromising. First, it doesn't do justice to Williamson's or Sosa's reports. On Chudnoff's view, there are phenomenological states $S_1, \ldots, S_n$ organized in some way such that his intuition is constituted by them. Williamson and Sosa, I assume, accept $S_1, \ldots, S_n$ as pre-doxastic antecedents to their inclinations in at least some cases. For instance, such antecedents are plausible in the development and description of the Gettier counterexamples, though it is significantly less clear what they are supposed to be in the case of the Naïve Comprehension Schema.[31] But even in what seem to be the best case scenarios for Chudnoff's proposal, such as the Gettier cases, the cognitive metaphysics is suspect. In considering the Gettier cases, the states to which Chudnoff alludes (thoughts, imaginings (imagery), intentions, beliefs, etc.) are seemingly spread out over development of the cases and not consciously attended to throughout. But our intuitions are not spread out over time in this way. And if they are not, they cannot be constituted by those events. Chudnoff, therefore, seems to be committed to the claim that these constituting states all occur consciously immediately prior to the formation of our resulting doxastic inclinations. But this does not correspond to the introspective situation Williamson or Sosa describes. Their complaint is a *paucity* of phenomenology objection. But Chudnoff's proposal requires, instead, a robust pre-doxastic phenomenology in which these thinkers fail to locate the relevant state even on reflection. If intuitions have a unique kind of proprietary phenomenology, it is unclear why being co-occurrent with other states (whether constituted by them or not) would make it

---

[31] Koksvik (2017) makes the important point that it is unclear on Chudnoff's view why presentational states have a common presentational phenomenology across different intuitions, given the diversity of cognitive antecedents that might be taken to constitute those intuitions.

so difficult to discover, even on careful introspective reflection and even when given guidance about what one is looking for (see Sytsma 2015 for related remarks).

One way to see this problem is to consider Williamson's (2020a, 232) response to Boghossian's (2020b, 223) claim that intuitions can be found with the help of theoretical guidance. Williamson writes, "He postulates that we can find such intellectual seemings in ourselves .... That is very different from actually finding them ... on the required occasions. For what they are worth, the results of my own attempted introspection are quite at odds with Boghossian's [and we may assume, Chudnoff's] postulate." I will return to this issue in Section 4, but for now, it is worth noting that at the very least, given Williamson's disavowal of being able to locate intuitions even with theoretical guidance, Chudnoff seems committed to denying that Williamson's intuitive beliefs are doxastically justified. This is because it is not sufficient for doxastic justification that one merely has an intuitional experience, as this would yield at most propositional justification. Rather, one's resulting beliefs must be appropriately based on it. Given that Williamson can't find the purported state, it seems that it can play at most a causal and not evidential role in his ensuing judgment (Moffett 2025).[32]

Koksvik (2017, 2021) has a more promising response. In his view, seemings (and so, intuitions) display a content-independent phenomenology of "pushiness". "An experience has phenomenology of pushiness if, instead of representing its content 'neutrally', or as a possibility for consideration, it 'pushes' the subject of the experience to accept its content, and this is an aspect of the very phenomenology of the experience" (2021, 71). Along with pushiness, Koksvik posits two further phenomenological features of seemings: objectivity and valence. Objectivity is that feature of intuitional experience that purports to be about objective, mind-independent *facts*. Objectivity captures essentially the same point made above about the presentationality of seemings, the apparent "presentness" ("in-the-worldness", "actuality") of their contents. For this reason, I will dub his view "pushy presentationality".[33]

---

[32] Ironically, Chudnoff's proposal is also at odds with the standard way many *defenders* of intuitions describe them. For my part, if intuitions are as Chudnoff describes them, then I, too, cannot locate them introspectively. Boghossian (2020a, 195–196), for instance, compares the experience of intuitions (intellectual seemings) with the experience of grasping puns and "garden path sentences". These "intellectual experiences" are surely not phenomenologically similar to the kind of state Chudnoff describes. They are rather immediate shifts in our grasp of things.

[33] Valence "reflects whether, when a subject enjoys an intuitional experience, the content of the experience seems true or false" (Koksvic 2017, 5). I will leave this feature to one side.

Pushy presentationality provides a more promising response to the Absent Intuition Problem because the hypothesized phenomenology of pushiness is at least a plausible candidate to confuse with the phenomenology of a conscious inclination to believe. In that case, Williamson might genuinely be aware of his intuition and base his belief on it, but simply misconceive the nature of that state as a disposition to believe. This is a Burge-style misconception of the intuition, and this kind of misconception is more plausibly compatible with Williamson being doxastically justified in his belief (Burge 1979).

There is a lot to be said for this idea. Seemings *are* in some sense pushy, and this pushiness is likely central to their epistemology. But the idea that there is a kind of "phenomenology of pushiness" is suspect in virtue of the fact that it is so similar to the phenomenology of doxastic inclinations. Consider Bengson's (2015a) functional claim that presentational states dispose us to believe. On this alternative view, there are two states: A presentational state and an (overridable) inclination to believe, to which the presentational state gives rise. On this two-state picture, we might want to say that the seeming functionally pushes us to accept the corresponding belief. But it is unclear why we should think there is any specific phenomenology associated with this functional property of seemings. Put differently, the pushiness of seemings isn't something different from their presentationality (Koksvik: objectivity), but rather a characterization of presentationality in terms of one of its characteristic effects. The associated phenomenology is the phenomenology of the inclination to believe, which is precisely the state Williamson isolates. And if that is so, then the phenomenology of doxastic inclinations swamps the phenomenology of intuitional presentationality, suggesting that the latter phenomenology is weak to non-existent.

3.4 ATP and the Absent Intuition Challenge

The Absent State Challenge ought to make defenders of intuitions reconsider reliance on the phenomenology of intuition and, in particular, on its epistemic significance. Ironically, however, we can co-opt this objection, not to call into question the existence of intuitions, but to establish their ubiquity. Consider our doxastic inclinations in the Gettier cases. Williamson acknowledges his awareness of "a conscious inclination to believe the Gettier proposition." In response to Boghossian, Williamson asks, "But how is one supposed to know whether one is in such a mysterious extra state? In my own case, for all introspection tells me, there is only the consciously inhibited disposition to judge [in the case of Naïve Comprehension]. Given . . . internalism . . . [i]f the difference between the presence and absence of the extra state of intuiting is not consciously available, it makes no difference to justification" (2020a, 212). Williamson is quite right about this commitment to internalism. But he is far less puzzled by the presence of his doxastic inclinations than he ought to be.[34]

What I will argue in this subsection is that Williamson is (in a broad, non-phenomenological sense) aware of this intuition, and this is evidenced by the fact that he, himself, takes his doxastic inclinations to be non-aberrant. So, my diagnosis of the Absent State Challenge is not that Williamson can't "find" his Gettier intuition; he can find it and actually bases his Gettier beliefs on it. Instead, he fails to reflectively appreciate a state that he has located because it is phenomenologically masked by a closely related state (his doxastic inclination) to which it gives rise, and which has a more robust phenomenology.

Suppose we take Williamson at his word and there is *nothing* else of which he is aware that accounts for this inclination: He considers the Gettier scenario and, subsequently, finds himself inclined to believe the Gettier proposition – an inclination which he, not inconsequentially, accepts. So described, Williamson seems to be suggesting that his "Gettier inclinations" (i.e., his inclinations to believe the Gettier proposition) are cognitively brute inclinations in the sense that he can give no relevant explanation of their presence other than consideration of the Gettier scenarios. After all, Williamson's Challenge is a *general* challenge to the presence of *any* antecedent phenomenologically conscious state that we could invoke to account for his doxastic inclinations, and not merely the absence, specifically, of an intuition.[35]

Now, brute inclinations are not themselves problematic. If I find myself inclined to a Hendricks martini, there is no felt need to understand from whence this inclination arises. But brute inclinations *to believe* are inherently problematic because it is in the nature of belief to aim at truth and, consequently, to be backed by reasons or to be otherwise rationally accounted for. For this reason, brute *doxastic* inclinations are cognitively alarming in much the way that intrusive thoughts are. Like an intrusive thought, having a brute doxastic inclination is reasonable grounds for believing that one has suffered some kind of cognitive aberration. Moreover, believing on the basis of such inclinations is flatly unjustified, and even badly irrational.

But our doxastic inclinations in the Gettier cases are nothing like this. The Gettier inclinations are clearly non-aberrant. On the contrary, they are routine, even banal, and we feel it is *prima facie* rational to give in to these inclinations. Moreover, there is also widespread (third-party) agreement that the resulting

---

[34] The point here is closely connected to what Bergmann (2006, 12) calls the "Subject's Perspective Objection".

[35] As an anonymous referee has pointed out, Williamson does acknowledge pre-doxastic states in considering the Gettier cases. However, he does not appear to think that any of these states rationalize his doxastic inclinations.

Gettier beliefs are justified when one does capitulate to them. Indeed, there has been almost universal acceptance of the Gettier propositions by philosophers, and the same is true for the target propositions of many or most important thought experiments.[36] None of these facts can be squared with Williamson's assertion that they are not based on any pre-doxastic states that rationalize them or our responses to them (see Bengson 2015a).

Williamson, of course, is not alone in this rhetoric. Machery, for instance, maintains that "When we consider the axiom of unrestricted comprehension, we have an inclination to judge that it is true, but this inclination is countervailed ... " (2017, 38). Machery doesn't explain *why* someone might be inclined to believe naïve comprehension in the first place or why doing so has any *prima facie* epistemic standing. In fact, he goes on to make this point in the case of perceptual seemings. Concerning the Müller-Lyre illusion, he says that the perceptual seeming is just an inclination to believe. He then asserts, "*Based on one's experience*, one is inclined to judge that the lines are unequal" (p. 38; emphasis added). Machery's instinct that the doxastic inclination needs to be based on some antecedent cognitive state is quite right. He goes wrong because he confuses which state is being put forward as analogous to an intuition. The analogous state is the perceptual experience and not something downstream from that, the inclination.[37] Properly understood, the perceptual case reinforces (rather than undermines) the need to posit an intuition to base one's doxastic inclinations on.

These considerations suggest that Williamson's claim that we are *aware* of nothing (relevant) beyond a conscious inclination to believe is mistaken. To adequately account for the first-person naturalness of our Gettier inclinations, there must be something in the antecedent cognitive environment generated by the thought experiment *of which we are consciously aware*. So, Williamson's "Gettier inclination" requires the presence of a pre-doxastic state that explains it and that serves to rationalize his subsequent belief. Weakly phenomenological (or non-phenomenological) intuitions provide us with something that can play this explanatory role consonantly with Williamson's general characterization of his *phenomenology*.

---

[36] This observation serves as the basis for Bealer's (1992) Starting Points Argument against empiricism, though with the (in this context) tendentious assumption that these beliefs are based on intuitions.

[37] Presumably, Machery wishes to distinguish perceptual experiences from perceptual seemings. While I reject this distinction, it leaves Machery's account of our perception-based doxastic inclinations in an awkward state of limbo. He rightly looks for an antecedent basis for these inclinations. He must then either follow the presentationalist in asserting that the experiences themselves function to generate and rationalize our perceptual inclinations – in which case, welcome aboard! Or he denies this. In which case, he, like Williamson, lacks an adequate account of the basis of our perceptual inclinations.

This point is similar to, but importantly different from, Boghossian's (2020b, 223) response. Boghossian distinguishes between states that are introspectively available without "theoretical guidance" and those that are introspectively available only with theoretical guidance; and he distinguishes both of these from states that are merely explanatory posits (and so not introspectively available at all). Boghossian takes intuitions to be in the middle category – available with guidance. This is wrong insofar as it implies that we don't have ready access to these states unless and until we turn our philosophical attention to locating them. If that were so, then our Gettier inclinations ought to initially strike us just as aberrantly as if we had no access to the intuitions at all. We could, at best, make sense of them only by way of *post hoc* investigation into our cognitive situation. But this does not accurately describe things. Our doxastic inclinations in these cases are first-person natural from the beginning, and this can only be explained if we take our introspective access to them to occur without the need for theoretical guidance.[38]

So, in contrast to Boghossian's view, the suggestion here is that we have *unguided* introspective access to the Gettier intuitions. The non-phenomenological theory of presentationality developed above concedes to Williamson that there is *no phenomenologically conscious* (certainly no phenomenologically salient) antecedent to the Gettier inclinations. What we "experience", consequently, is the phenomenology of those inclinations – just as Williamson reports. Williamson errs in thinking that since he "has no such *feelings* about [his] inclinations to judge" (2020b, 233; emphasis added), there is, therefore, no presentational state to which he has access. This is what the non-phenomenological theory of seemings rejects. But Williamson – perhaps caught in the throes of his own epistemological theorizing – fails to take account of the phenomenology we straightforwardly *do* experience, not merely the existence of *but the felt non-aberrancy* of his inclinations. Williamson even concedes that "[w]hat matters is why I favor p in the first place" (2020b, 233). But his own theory is inadequate to account for this, leaving it as an unexplained fact of our psychology.[39] For my part, I find the idea that we possess brute, yet rational, inclinations to believe far more mysterious and normatively problematic than any proposed theory of intuitions.

---

[38] Boghossian observes that in "our typical responses to classical thought experiments [our] inclinations don't feel as though they are coming out of the blue .... They present themselves as based on their seeming true" (2020b, 224). My point about the first-person naturalness of our Gettier inclinations is effectively the same as Boghossian's initial point here. But the claim that the inclinations *present themselves* as based on seemings (presentational states) is, in my view a mistake as I discuss below.

[39] Interestingly, reliabilism (e.g., Lyons 2009) is unable to account for this point either.

Before considering possible alternatives, let me summarize. These observations establish the need for something to explain two quite familiar epistemic and cognitive features of philosophical thought experiments, which are not generally in dispute:

- The presence of *non-aberrant* doxastic inclinations that do not arise from any phenomenologically salient antecedent state or states.
- The *prima facie* reasonableness (both from the first-person and third-person perspectives) of giving in to those inclinations.[40]

It is incumbent on any philosopher who denies that these explanations go by way of intuitions to give an alternative account of them. And whatever else we may say about this case, these inclinations are plainly not generated by perceptual or introspective states. Consequently, whatever state we invoke here must behave functionally the way intuitions are claimed to function in at least these two respects. Given this, the defender of intuitions might well claim to have established the main goal of "rationalist epistemology" already, namely, the existence of a source of basic, non-experiential evidence (reasons). What remains are merely internal disputes about their nature. It is also worth remarking that a non-phenomenological theory of intuitions does not require phenomenology, which may help account for the accusation that they are "mysterious". For if intuitions were phenomenologically salient in the way perceptual experiences are, there would be no controversy over their existence but merely over their nature.

Once we unshackle the theory of intuitions from the effort to isolate an elusive "phenomenology of intuition", we can cast a much broader net in understanding their role in our cognitive and epistemic lives. Again, my claim here is not that intuitions are merely theoretical posits whose existence can only be inferred from their characteristic doxastic and epistemic effects. That view is inconsistent with the preceding points. The claim is rather that these features of standard thought experiments should make us sensitive to the presence of an intuition to which we have non-phenomenological conscious access, but which is often phenomenologically masked or overlooked.

There are two plausible alternatives to positing intuitions in these cases: (1) The tired old crutch of positing "quick and dirty" inferences, and (2) an appeal

---

[40] These features are closely related to two of the central features that Bengson isolates in his discussion of presentational states: "Presentational states do not merely dispose or incline assent; they also seem to rationalize such assent, in the (psychological) sense that they tend to make formation of corresponding beliefs seem rational or fitting from the first-person perspective" (2015a, 723). I take it that by qualifying "rationalize" with 'in the psychological sense ....'" Bengson intends to be invoking motivating reasons. This leaves it open as to whether presentational states are also normative reasons, viz., count in favor of so-believing. I take it that they are (Moffett 2025).

to "concept application" in lieu of an appeal to intuition. I will put off a discussion of inference until Section 4.3, where I consider it in detail. There, I will argue that inference essentially involves the use of intuitions. If so, then the effort to avoid invoking intuitions in the case of thought experiments by appealing to inference is a non-starter. In addition, once I have developed a theory of inference, I will argue that the way in which we form beliefs on the basis of thought experiments is different from the way in which we form beliefs on the basis of inference. So, I will begin by focusing on the appeal to concept application.

4 Intuition and Concept Application

4.1 Concept Application & Modal Force

Williamson says: "Our belief in the Gettier proposition depends on our capacity to apply epistemological concepts online to encountered instances, *our general capacity to apply concepts* we can apply online offline too, in the imagination, and our capacity to use such imaginative exercises to evaluate counterfactual conditionals. ... " (2007, 216).[41] He goes on to suggest that the difference between those who "respond correctly" to the Gettier case is that they are more skillful in applying concepts than those who do not. He then concludes that "[t]hese paradigms [of the reliance on intuitions] provide no evidence of intellectual seemings, if the phrase is supposed to mean anything more than intuitions [as beliefs or inclinations to believe]" (p. 217).

However, while Williamson's discussion lacks detail, it gestures at a possible response to the arguments of the preceding section. Specifically, Williamson's appeal to concept application suggests that the non-aberrancy of our doxastic inclinations in relevant cases might result, not because those inclinations are based on intuitions, but because they are based on the (hopefully skillful) application of concepts.

The attraction of this deflationary appeal to concept application over intuition presumably derives from a pre-critical sense that concept application involves positing no metaphysically queer cognitive faculties, the way intuition (purportedly) does. After all, concept application is something that even die-hard anti-intuition philosophers agree occurs generally and ubiquitously. Thus, if we can simply reduce intuitions to or eliminate them in favor of acts of concept application, we will seemingly have gone a long way toward demystifying our epistemology. Moreover, unlike "intellectual seemings", acts

---

[41] Presumably, by "evaluate counterfactual conditionals," Williamson means "evaluate their truth value," and presumably he intends this to also involve concept application.

of concept application carry no overt or presumed commitment to a dubious cognitive phenomenology.

But the appeal to concept application is by no means a panacea for intuition skeptics. First, if an appeal to concept application is to usurp the position of intuition, it must take on the burdens of that position: Applying a concept must account for the non-aberrancy and normative reasonableness of downstream inclinations and beliefs. Second, it must be consistent with Williamson's (general) challenge that he is not introspectively aware of any relevant antecedents to his doxastic inclinations. Finally, it must achieve this without tacit appeal to intuitions or collapsing into a theory of intuitions (in either case, a Pyrrhic victory).

I will argue that this cannot be done. To apply a concept is to act in a certain way. So, the Williamsonian idea would be that our being justified in believing the Gettier propositions depends in some crucial way on our skillful (i.e., accurate) application of various epistemological concepts (e.g., knowledge, justification). This is something that advocates of intuitions can and do embrace. Bealer, for instance, characterizes philosophical "thought experiments" thus: "[Most philosophical appeals to intuition involve] the evidential use of intuitions about certain possibilities and *about whether relevant concepts apply to those possibilities.*" (1996a, 4; emphasis added). On Bealer's view, concept application presupposes, and does not supersede, an appeal to intuition. Strawson, in his comments on Bealer (1992), suggests the point extends generally: "[Bealer's] argument turns largely ... on the fact that certain concepts occur essentially in the statement of [empiricism], concepts such as those of 'experience', 'observation', 'evidence', 'simplest', 'justified', 'explanation'; and Bealer argues that, in order for these concepts to be applied in any particular case, recourse must be had to 'intuitions' about what counts as falling under any of these concepts. The point seems well taken: ... But, surely, not only of these. We have majestic authority for the view that the co-operation of understanding, the faculty of concepts, is required for the recognition of whatever we recognize as falling under any concept whatever" (1992, 141).[42]

One reason to think the Bealer-Strawson theory of concept application is right concerns the "modal force" of intuitions, or rather the associated doxastic inclinations, which I will exploit to argue for the connection between concept application and intuition. In characterizing our standard justificatory procedure, Bealer observes that "when we have an a priori intuition, say, that if P then not not P, this presents itself as necessary" (1996a, 5). Bealer takes the "modal

---

[42] It might be useful to distinguish concept application in the sense intended here from mere predication.

force" of our intuitions to indicate that they present metaphysically necessary truths. He proceeds to tentatively assert an analysis along the following lines: "I am unsure how to analyze what is meant by saying that an a priori intuition presents itself as necessary. Perhaps something like this: necessarily, if x intuits that P, it seems to x that P and also that necessarily P. But I wish to take no stand on this" (p. 5). That is:

$\Box((x$ has an *a priori* intuition that p$) \rightarrow$ (it seems to x that p & it seems to x that $\Box$p$))$.

Since $\Box$p $\rightarrow$ p, the right-hand side of this formulation may strike us as unduly complex. Presumably, however, Bealer is trying to capture the fact that in cases like Gettier's, we have the sense that our intuition directly involves the non-modal propositions (e.g., that Smith is justified and that Smith doesn't know). This also accords most naturally with treating intuition as an immediate justifier of the corresponding non-modal belief and not something that we arrive at inferentially (*via* box elimination).

But Bealer's diagnosis of the modal force of propositions is problematic. Consider the case of thought experiments (unlike the case of double negation he considers). In these cases, the target proposition itself is not necessary. Consequently, on Bealer's treatment, the intuition in question would have to be something like the following, where C is the description of the relevant thought experiment:

$\Box((x$ has an *a priori* intuition that p$) \rightarrow$ (it seems to x that p & it seems to x that $\Box(C \rightarrow p))$.

While the second conjunct of this proposal may be intuitive, it does not strike me as the correct way of thinking about how naïve subjects encounter, for example, the Gettier cases. It is especially awkward for real-world cases of thought experiments.

Moreover, the non-modal conjunct of the Gettier intuition and the proposed modal conjunct can come apart in ways that don't seem relevant to the justificatory nature of intuitions and which are, in any event, at odds with the basic framework of Presentationalism. After all, insofar as we think that these intuitions depend in some central way on our grasp of the relevant concepts, there is no clear reason why we couldn't have a Burge-like misunderstanding or incomplete understanding in our grasp of the concept of METAPHYSICAL NECESSITY while still having the non-modal Gettier intuition given in the first conjunct. It is certainly not obvious that confusion involving the concept of METAPHYSICAL NECESSITY would preclude our having intuitions about the concept of JUSTIFICATION in this case.

Pust aims to capture the modal force of intuitions in a way that respects our sense that the content of our intuitions is not modally loaded in the way Bealer's proposal suggests:

> S has a rational intuition that p [at t] if and only if (a) S has a purely intellectual experience [at t], when considering the question of whether p, that p; and (b) at t, if S were to consider whether p is necessarily true, then S would have a purely intellectual experience that necessarily p (2000, 9).

While Pust's condition (b) separates out the modal and non-modal features of intuitions, it overshoots: The subjunctive analysis does not adequately capture the fact that we are aware of this sense of necessity in considering such cases.[43]

In my view, these accounts of the modal force of intuitions in terms of modal content miss a crucial insight. The sense of necessity we have in the Gettier case is not a sense of metaphysical necessity, but of *deontic necessity*. And it is not characteristic of our intuitions proper, but of our understanding of where our doxastic inclinations come from. That is, the Gettier inclinations seem to us to arise from the intuition that a certain judgment is *conceptually required or conceptually mandated* in the situation being considered.[44] Compare the following two questions about Gettier's scenario:

(A) We consider the Gettier scenario and the question of whether Smith is justified in believing that either Jones owns a Ford or Brown is in Barcelona. We find a determinate answer: Smith is justified, as *required* by the conditions specified in the scenario.[45]

(B) We consider the Gettier scenario and the question of whether Smith and Jones are friends but not *very* close friends. Here we find that the answer is not determinate. To be sure, there is evidence that Smith and Jones are not very close friends, and this evidence might incline us to believe they are not. But the truth of this proposition is not required by Gettier's description of the case.

In (A), we are conscious that the basis of our doxastic inclination (and subsequent judgment) is conceptual and not, as it is in (B), inferential. The sense of deontic necessity arises from our introspective awareness of the intellectual basis

---

[43] Pust's condition (b) also seems inadequate for the same reasons proffered against Bealer's proposal. If S has a Burge-like confusion about the concept of metaphysical necessity, it is not obvious that the proposed counterfactual is true. For instance, if S is conceptually confused about metaphysical necessity, it is not obvious that in the nearest possible worlds in which S considers whether □p, S would have a purely intellectual experience that □p.

[44] This claim falls short of Boghossian's (2020b) claim that our doxastic inclinations in thought experiments present *themselves* as being based on seemings. It is rather the weaker claim that *introspection* presents such inclinations as conceptually required.

[45] Likewise, the Gettier scenario is fully determinate with respect to the concept of knowledge: We find a determinate answer, Smith does not know, is *required* by the conditions specified in G2.

of our doxastic inclinations.[46] This way of addressing the Absent Intuition Challenge turns on the idea that Williamson and Sosa conflate the phenomenological absence of intuition with their introspective absence. Unlike Chudnoff's view discussed above, these philosophers do not fail to find an intuition (the non-aberrancy of their beliefs establishes this) but rather display a metacognitive failure to recognize what they have clearly found. This metacognitive failure may benefit from what Boghossian calls "theoretical guidance", but such guidance is not necessary for first-order, non-phenomenological access to those intuitions. Because it will be relevant later, a similar point can be made concerning Malmgren's (2018, 228–229) claim that the etiology of our Gettier judgments is "subjectively opaque". I reject this. In my opinion, the Gettier cases (and other thought experiments) are generally not hard cases in the penumbra of inferential/non-inferential. They are clearly non-inferential judgments. I will return to this point in Section 4.2.

In sum, reflecting on the felt deontic force of our doxastic inclinations in thought experiments provides reason to think that we have non-phenomenal awareness of a pre-doxastic intuition which rationalizes those inclinations. Call these *intuition-based doxastic inclinations*. Basic concept application may then be analyzed as a judgment made in response to an intuition-based doxastic inclination.[47] This proposal nicely captures Williamson's claim that concept application is a kind of skillful action (i.e., something over which we exercise control). Moreover, this means that we cannot eschew the role of intuitions here in favor of unconscious (subpersonal) mechanisms of concept application. For such mechanisms, being unconscious cannot explain the deontic force of those

---

[46] Pust comes close to this point by calling these states baseless "purely intellectual experience[s]".

[47] The qualifier "basic" is intended to circumvent the objection that every belief involves concept application. If, for instance, I come to believe that platypuses are mammals on the basis of testimony, there is surely some sense in which I apply the concept of being a mammal to platypuses. This sense of concept application, however, clearly differs from the sort discussed in the text. It might be better to simply call it "concept predication".

An anonymous referee for Cambridge objects here that this view is problematic because (a) animals (e.g., rats) apply concepts, but (b) rats don't have intuitions. The empirical claim in (a) about rats is not uncontroversial, though I accept it (for overviews see Andrews 2020, Ch. 5; Beck 2012). Specifically, I grant that there is a nominal sense in which rats possess concepts and have assertive representations and so, correlatively, a nominal sense in which they "apply" those concepts. I am doubtful, however, that they apply concepts in the sense in which this behavior underwrites the normative evaluation of these actions that is needed in order to respond to the arguments given in the text. And if they do, then I am willing to accept that they also have intuitions. If that strikes the reader as far-fetched, they may be overly intellectualizing what intuitions are – which would not be surprising given the sophisticated conceptual structure of many theories of intuitions (not to mention perceptions). One of the strengths of the view developed here is that it does not require that sort of sophisticated cognitive machinery and so does not obviously preclude intuitions from occurring in concept-possessing, non-human animals. But this debate in cognitive ethology cannot be taken up here.

inclinations as described above or their non-aberrancy. An adequate account of the Gettier inclinations has to steer a very narrow course through the Charybdis of non-aberrancy and the Scylla of the Absent State Challenge. It is my contention that only phenomenologically masked (or a-phenomenological) intuitions can navigate these waters successfully.

Before drawing out some important implications of the preceding defense of intuition-based concept application, it will be useful to provide a detailed picture of how concrete-case intuitions function in thought experiments.

4.2 Thought Experiments & Concrete Case Intuitions

Although the use of thought experiments is ubiquitous in philosophy, there is surprisingly little agreement about their mechanics. Williamson, for instance, characterizes the Gettier belief thus:

> "If a thinker were Gettier-related to a proposition, [they] would have a justified true belief in it without knowledge" (2004, 195).

Now, I think that this counterfactual is unquestionably *not* the proposition that advocates of intuitions would put forward as the Gettier intuition. It is, rather, a logical consequence of some combination of propositions they regard as stipulated in the thought experiment and propositions they find intuitive given those stipulations.[48] This is not to claim that Williamson's counterfactual lacks intuitive support; a well-versed philosopher paying close attention would likely find it intuitive. However, general propositions like this are not our most secure evidential basis, and Williamson's description of the Gettier argument tends to obscure the nature of the intuitions involved.

Describing what he calls the standard justificatory procedure, Bealer characterizes philosophical "thought experiments" thus:[49] "[I]t is intuitions about concrete cases that are accorded primary evidential weight by our standard justificatory procedure; theoretical intuitions are by comparison given far less evidential weight" (1996a, 4). The suggestion is that thought experiments involve (or at least should involve) something like the following process: (1) The consideration of (describing of, imagining of) a certain "concrete" scenario;

---

[48] For a similar discussion, see Hetherington (2011, 121).
[49] Bealer (p. 5) objects to calling the hypothetical scenarios deployed in philosophy "thought experiments" because it tends to blur the differences between them and empirically oriented thought experiments (as in, e.g., the Newton-Leibniz debate over the nature of space), which involve "physical intuitions", not a priori intuitions. The physical intuitions involved in traditional thought experiments do not present with the force of necessity characteristic of a priori intuitions (see below). While it is important to keep this difference in mind, the use of "thought experiment" to characterize philosophical cases is now so entrenched that it seems futile to buck this trend, and there is no alternative, readily available vocabulary for succinct communication.

(2) Canvassing an intuition as to whether that this scenario is possible; and finally (3) canvassing an intuition as to whether certain unstipulated target concepts must apply in that case.

The scenarios involved in step (1) are concrete in that they involve specific (though possibly imaginary) entities having the specific properties and relations stipulated in the description of the case. Let us agree to call the set of stipulated "propositions" in Gettier's second case, G2. So G2 will include "propositions" like:

- Smith has strong evidence that Jones owns a Ford.
- Jones does not own a Ford.
- Brown is currently in Barcelona.
- Smith does not know Brown's current location, etc.

The propositions in this case are held suppositionally rather than, for example, assertively. Extending our earlier symbolic shorthand, we can represent this suppositional attitude as ⊩ G2 (x supposes that G2). By contrast, if we understood Gettier's examples to be reports of actual events (i.e., to describe a real-world Gettier case), our attitude toward G2 would be assertive: ⊢ G2 (x believes that G2). As we will see, this difference in our cognitive posture towards G2 makes no difference with respect to the philosophical upshot of the Gettier propositions.

Scenarios such as G2 are, of course, inherently partial. Despite this, few of us have any difficulty concluding that G2 is metaphysically possible (viz., ⊢ ◇G2). This conclusion is arguably based on an intuition: Upon considering G2, it seems to us that ◇G2 (viz., ⊣ ◇G2). Indeed, it is arguable that what Bealer calls above "intuitions about possibilities" are just intuitions about the applicability of the concept of metaphysical possibility to a considered scenario. I do not want to insist on this claim, however.

Once the modal acceptability of G2 is recognized, we arrive at step (3) – establishing whether certain "target" concepts apply in that scenario. In the second Gettier case, there are two target propositions:

a. Whether Smith is justified in believing that either Jones owns a Ford or Brown is in Barcelona
b. Whether Smith knows that either Jones owns a Ford or Brown is in Barcelona.

When we think of "the Gettier proposition," it is (b) that we typically have front of mind. But obviously, for the counterexample to go through, (a) needs to be established as well. According to Bealer, (a) and (b) are settled by intuitions about whether certain concepts (JUSTIFICATION, KNOWLEDGE) apply in the described scenario.[50]

It will be worth considering this proposal in a bit of detail, for careful development of the mechanics of thought experiments will help us to differentiate them from cases of inference. Let us symbolize the target proposition in (a) above as J, and the target proposition in (b) as K. Now given what was said above about the content of intuitions (and resulting doxastic inclinations), one might think that the Gettier intuitions will simply be straight intuitions that J (i.e., ⊣ J) and not K (⊣ ¬K). While this is not wrong, it is inherently partial since it doesn't do justice to the fact that we are supposing, rather than asserting, G2 (i.e., ⊩ G2). Unlike what we might think of as a pure or context-independent intuition (e.g., a basic principle of logic), the intuitions that J and ¬K arise only against a backdrop of supposing that things are a certain way. Let us symbolize this dependency of our intuition on our suppositions as in (c) below, where the | should be understood as the cognitive context in which the intuition occurs. (Although the cognitive context typically will be consciously accessible to the subject, there is no presumption that it is the focus of the subject's attention or that the subject must be aware of its role in generating her intuition.) Compare (c) to something closer to Williamson's proposed picture of the Gettier intuition, which we could represent as in (d):

c. ⊩ G2 | ⊣ J (viz., x supposes that G2 and in that context it seems to them that J)
d. | ⊣ G2 → J (viz., It seems to x that G2 implies (or entails) J.

The problem with taking the Gettier intuition to be the presentation of the conditional posited in (d) can be seen most clearly in "real world" Gettier cases (i.e., cases which we believe to be Gettier contexts to obtain). In such cases, we seem to be able to judge that J (or ¬K) only inferentially:

1. | ⊣ G2 → J   [Assumption]
2. ⊢ G2 → J   [By Moderate dogmatism]
3. ⊢ G2   [Assumption of real-world Gettier case]
4. Therefore, ⊢ J   2,3

But this inferential route is contrived. Applying a concept in a context isn't a matter of it seeming that the context-independent conditional holds, accepting

---

[50] Settling these questions is not a matter of first having a general theoretical intuition that establishes a general principle and then deriving these specific claims from it. Rather, we settle the specific cases directly. For example, we do not first consider a claim like: If x were justified in believing that p and x were to infer (p ∨ q) from p and x had no reason to believe q, then x would be justified in believing (p ∨ q). Finding this to be intuitively plausible, we then infer that (a) should be answered affirmatively as an implication of this general principle. Introspectively, this seems exactly right.

that we are in that context, and then inferring the consequent. The payoff of appealing to concept application is that it gives us a direct (non-inferential) route to the application of the concept in the context.[51] This is what (c) captures. It tells us that if we suppose Smith to be in the "Gettier condition" ($\Vdash$ G2), this will generate the Gettier intuitions ($\dashv$ J, $\dashv$ ¬K). As a result, our *prima facie* justification for accepting J and ¬K follows in accordance with MD.

The suppositional attitude is in important respects more like an assertive attitude ($\vdash$ G2) than like an attitude of mere consideration (– G2) (Myers 2024). We might call it a "pseudo-assertive" attitude. In particular, the suppositional attitude functions as a context that generates *genuine* intuitions. This phenomenon is not distinctive of philosophical thought experiments. Our intuitive responses to thought experiments are of a piece with the general phenomenon of imaginative engagement, in which we have genuine cognitive and emotional responses to scenarios known to be fictional (see, e.g., Camp 2017). The difference between the suppositional and assertive attitudes toward G2 doesn't lie in their capacity to generate intuitions, but instead in their differential impacts with respect to MD. Specifically, an intuition driven by a suppositional attitude has a pre-emptive defeater – our awareness of the fact that it is based on a supposition. Consequently, any *prima facie* justification for believing outright on the basis of such intuitions does not go through. This would be analogous to the situation in which someone knowingly enters a highly realistic virtual reality scenario – the presentationality of the perceptual experiences will not justify a corresponding judgment because it is pre-emptively defeated by our awareness of the pretense.

But if the intuitions generated by thought experiments don't justify the corresponding Gettier beliefs *via* MD, how do thought experiments work? We can reconstruct an answer along the following lines: The thought experiment proceeds by producing a stepwise sequence of intuitions and other cognitive states, which start with the consideration of the Gettier context. This generates a possibility intuition that G2 is possible ($\dashv \Diamond$G2). Given this possibility intuition, we are licensed to *suppose* that G2 holds. This supposition then yields the corresponding Gettier intuitions ($\dashv$ J, $\dashv$ ¬K). As we have seen, the Gettier intuitions are conceptually required by the supposition of G2: Assuming G2, J and ¬K seem conceptually required. Once this sequence of individual intuitions is generated, they *jointly* form a cognitive context in which a fourth and final intuition – their joint possibility – is generated. Schematically:

1. – G2 | $\dashv \Diamond$G2
2. $\Vdash$ G2 | $\dashv$ J
3. $\Vdash$ G2 | $\dashv$ ¬K

---

[51] This is not to deny that in underspecified cases, we might arrive at such a conclusion inferentially.

4. $(- G2 \mid \dashv \Diamond G2 \ \& \Vdash G2 \mid \dashv J \ \& \Vdash G2 \mid \dashv \neg K) \mid \dashv \Diamond G2+J+\neg K$
5. $\vdash \Diamond(G2+J+\neg K)$ 4, MD

(5) is justified *via* an application of MD. And since G2+J+¬K is a counterexample to the traditional analysis of knowledge, we conclude that justified, true belief is not sufficient for knowledge.[52]

There are two crucial features to this characterization of thought experiments. First, even though our intuitions are dependent on other cognitive states, in hypothetical cases, those states themselves do not require or even allow epistemic justification. For this reason, the justification for (5) is both *a priori* and foundational.

Second, this treatment of concrete-case intuitions draws a sharp distinction between the cognitive conditions that generate intuitions (the material preceding the vertical stroke) and their contents. So, (1)-(5) does not articulate an *argument* for (5) in which the subject consciously invokes the antecedent beliefs and seemings in order to make certain transitions. Instead, (1)-(5) describe a sequence of rationally ordered cognitive states that the subject undergoes. As a result, the reason for accepting (5) is given directly by MD: Since it seems to us that $\Diamond$G2+J+¬K, we are *prima facie* justified in accepting that it is possible.[53] In this sense, our concrete-case intuitions are only cognitively, and not epistemically, dependent on the apprehensions which generate them. Instead, the epistemic significance of our (hypothetical) intuitions is *fully* located, as it should be, in their presentational nature.

In Section 3, I argued that concept application involves intuitions. If that conclusion is correct, there should be little doubt about the indispensability and ubiquity of intuitions, for concept application is both indispensable and ubiquitous. In this closing section, I will consider two case studies, inference and perception, and argue that both involve concept application and so intuition. The goal is to establish the centrality of intuitions in the case of ordinary *empirical* knowledge, both commonsensical and scientific. The role of intuitions in these cases, I will argue, is not indirect in the sense of establishing *a priori* background principles on which our empirical knowledge ultimately depends. Instead, instances of intuition play a direct role in all (or almost all) cases of inference and perception.

---

[52] Recall that in G2 it is stipulated that Smith truly believes that either Jones owns a Ford or Brown is in Barcelona.

[53] This allows us to avoid treating intuitions as being about complex conditionals of the sort Williamson invokes.

4.3 Inference & Concept Application

Arguably, inference (the *act* of inferring) involves concept application intuitions. But the epistemic role of intuitions in inference is different from the role they play in the justification of foundational belief. This is because our intuitions are not acting as premises (reasons) in support of the conclusion (Chudnoff 2024; Huemer 2016, 152) nor, on pain of regress, are they justifying beliefs that act as premises (Boghossian 2014). Instead, they serve as a necessary condition for doxastic transitions to count as genuine inferential acts resulting in justified beliefs.

One argument for this claim is what I have called elsewhere the Argument from Agency (Moffett 2023). Let P be a set of beliefs and C be some further belief that I have formed "on the basis" of P. It is not sufficient for this transition to count as an inferential act that P merely causes C. As Broome says, "When you reason, your premise attitudes cause your conclusion attitude. But reasoning is not *merely* a causal process. Somehow, you do it" (2013, 237). One way of marking Broome's point is that actions are typically creditable to the subject, rather than to a subsystem of the subject (Jones 2017). Inference is something that I do and, moreover, something I do for reasons.

Arruda and Povinelli (2018, 450) identify two ways for an agent to relate to her reasons. When an agent stands in the endorsement relation to her reasons, she acts in light of a reason of which she is aware, and she endorses it as a motivating reason. When an agent stands in the directed relation to her reasons, the agent relates to those reasons to the extent that she accepts the background attitudes that influence her actions as her attitudes; and her actions are such that she could pair her actions with explicit reasons for action, but she does not. The Argument from Agency claims that, on either expression of agency, our beliefs are inferentially justified only if the subject relies on corresponding concept application intuitions.

Consider, first, the expression of agency by way of the endorsement relation. (Call this type of agency "endorsement agency".) In the case of inference, this would consist of paradigmatic cases of fully explicit inference. Such cases clearly entail *categorizing* some beliefs (or their contents) as reasons; that is, as being the sorts of things that can be counted among our reasons for inferring something. If the subject did not categorize them as reasons, she could hardly be counted as having explicitly *inferred* something from them in the sense of inferring associated with the endorsement relation. So, when my inference from P to C is an expression of my endorsement agency, I will need to have corresponding concept application intuitions to the effect that P is a reason. These intuitions are a necessary precondition for my inferring from P to C and so a necessary condition for C's being justified on the basis of such an inference.

The preceding argument does not turn on any detailed theory of inference and, in particular, does not turn on acceptance of Boghossian's much-discussed Taking Condition (2014):

The Taking Condition: Inferring necessarily involves the thinker taking his premises to [epistemically] support his conclusion and drawing his conclusion because of that fact.

It is, however, consistent with this requirement when analyzed as an intuition (Chudnoff 2024; Huemer 2016). If it is thought that, in explicit inference, one must bring the doxastic transition under the concept of epistemic support, then inferences involving endorsement agency will require the corresponding intuition. Personally, it strikes me as very likely that it will for two reasons: (1) the agent must understand their action as involving epistemic, rather than prudential, support, and (2) it seems unlikely that in inferring we would deploy the concept of reasons (and the correlative concept of a conclusion) without deploying the concept of epistemic support. But for my purposes, I will not defend that more robust role of intuitions here. Establishing the necessity of applying the concept of reasons is sufficient to make the point.

Of course, recent work on inference has gone into arguing that explicit inference of the sort that involves endorsement agency is rare. Much of this work targets Inferential Internalism generally, and the Taking Condition in particular. Consider, for instance, Smithies' (2024, 133) bike-riding example: "Suppose you learn that the weather forecast predicts rain tomorrow and this prompts you to wonder whether your friend will cancel the bike ride that you planned together. Conscious thought might be needed to figure out how your friend will react to the weather forecast. But once you decide that they will cancel if it rains, and you already know that it will rain, you don't need to consider whether these premises support the conclusion that the ride will be cancelled." This last claim may be true, but it isn't obvious that this is a counterexample to the Taking Condition. This is because, in *wondering* how your friend will react to rain, you have already taken yourself to be looking for things that support believing that they will have some reaction. Rather than being a case of inference without the taking condition, this is a case in which the purpose is to find something we take to support one of a given set of propositional alternatives.[54] But even if we grant that this is a case of inference without the Taking Condition, it is still an expression of endorsement agency and, as such, requires application of the concept of

---

[54] On the semantics of rogative verbs like "wonder" see Theiler et al. 2017. Friedman (2019, 298), for instance, characterizes inquiry of the sort invoked in Smithies' example as "aiming to figure something out".

reasons (among others).[55] You must take your belief that if it rains, your friend will cancel, for instance, as a reason.

More radical cases, however, do seem to correspond to reason-directed agency, the kind of agency involved with the directedness relation. Smithies, for instance, adapts his bike riding example to be a case of "unconscious" inference: One night, you might go to bed wondering how your friend will react to the forecast of rain tomorrow. Without resolving it, you wake up the next morning already knowing that they will cancel. There is a wide range of such cases of having the answer to a problem "come to you" after putting aside explicit consideration of the problem for some period of time. Treating them as involving reason-directed agency allows us to categorize them as actions, and specifically, inferential acts. As Arruda and Povinelli note, with perhaps some liberalization on the conditions, the directed relation will also account for inferences in animals and very young children.

Unlike the endorsement cases, however, I am skeptical that reason-directed inferences are, on their own, able to transmit justification. The problem, at least from the internalist point of view adopted here, is that from the subject's point of view, the conclusion beliefs are no better than premonitions or hunches. That is, reason-directed inferences run afoul of Bergmann's Subject's Perspective Objection.[56]

SPO: If the subject holding a belief isn't aware of what that belief has going for it, then she isn't aware of how its status is any different from a stray hunch

---

[55] Cases like Siegel's (2019, 18) Kindness case are arguably too extreme. In this case, we are to imagine that in observing the interaction of a post office clerk with a customer, it strikes us that the clerk is kind, even though we cannot identify what it is about the clerk that leads to this thought. In such cases, we would normally report something like this: "There was *something* about the clerk that seemed kind." Such cases are, in my view, best treated as cases of "enhanced" perceptual seemings (perceptually, the clerk seemed kind) with the resulting belief being justified by a straightforward application of MD. (For an initial sketch of "enhanced" perceptual states, see Section 4.4 below.) Such cases would not count as even reason-directed inference because the underlying states that generated the belief are not ones that the subject accepts as their own.

[56] Taylor and Coppenger extend the SPO in defense of inferential internalism and the Taking Condition.

> **Inferential SPO:** If the subject holding an inferential belief isn't *aware* of the connection between her evidence and her inferential belief, then she isn't *aware* of how her evidence's bearing on that belief is any different than its bearing on a stray hunch or arbitrary conviction. From that we may conclude that *from her perspective it is an accident* that her inferential belief is true and that implies that it isn't a justified belief (2024, 199).

> Accepting their arguments, which seem to me correct, would extend the role of intuitions in inference. But for the purposes of defending the role of intuitions in inference, SPO is sufficient.

or an arbitrary conviction. From that, we may conclude that from her perspective, it is an accident that her belief is true. And that implies that it isn't a justified belief

(2016, 12).

Suppose I am justified in believing that my friend will cancel our ride if it rains and that it will rain tomorrow. At some point in the day (without explicit consideration), it occurs to me as a result of a reason-directed inference that my friend will cancel.[57] The question is: At that moment, is my belief doxastically justified simply in virtue of my reason-directed inference (together with the justification for my premise beliefs)? It seems to me that it is not. To see this, simply imagine the case as one in which it doesn't immediately occur to you that your conclusion belief is the answer to a question you had been pondering earlier in the day. In that case, you simply find yourself having a certain belief about the future (that your friend will cancel), but you have no understanding of its basis. It is in this sense that the conclusion belief is like a premonition or hunch. It isn't until you subsequently recognize the reasons for the conclusion that it is, as Pryor (2005, 203) puts it, "epistemically appropriate" for you to believe the conclusion.[58] Of course, in many cases of the sort Smithies' is describing, no such delay occurs. Because by hypothesis the background beliefs are ours, we quickly locate them and recognize their bearing on the belief that has come to us. But that doesn't mean that the justification arises from the inference alone; instead, it serves to motivate us to find an explanation for our otherwise epistemically untethered conviction.[59] But in doing so, we will again need to categorize our beliefs as reasons, and so we will need to deploy concept application intuitions.

Summarizing: Either our inferential acts involve the endorsement relation to our reasons or the directedness relation. The endorsement relation entails

---

[57] In Smithies' description, I find myself *knowing* that my friend will cancel. But such a description prejudges the question I am asking and doesn't seem correct unless we are using "knowing" in the sense of "feeling subjectively confident in believing". My own sense of the case is that I come to have a strong inclination to judge that my friend will cancel. But in that case, we don't have an inference from our premises to our conclusion (since an inclination to believe is not a conclusion). So perhaps the most neutral way of describing the case is one in which I just find myself believing that my friend will cancel.

[58] The surprising conclusion is that doxastic justification (and, so, basing) requires not just more than a causal basing relation, but more than just any agentive causal basing relation. Instead, it requires the kind of endorsement relation that occurs in explicit inference.

It is possible that in reason-directed inferences, the subject must recognize her belief as a conclusion. If so, then this will already involve concept application intuitions.

[59] This is not to deny that we can be held responsible for the conclusions and beliefs. In response to Richard's (2019) example of beliefs formed by implicit bias, Boghossian (2019, 120) points out that all this shows is that we can be held responsible for our beliefs, independent of their origin.

categorizing some of our beliefs as reasons and so (by Section 4.1) presupposes the use of concept application intuitions. So, intuitions are necessary for inferential justification *via* expression of our endorsement agency. The directedness relation does not entail categorizing our beliefs as reasons. However, reason-directed inferences do not justify the conclusion until we subsequently identify the reasons for the conclusion. So, intuitions are necessary for inferential justification *via* expression of our reason-directed agency. So, intuitions are necessary for inferential justification.

This function of intuitions also helps differentiate inferences from the non-inferential beliefs formed in thought experiments: In thought experiments, we do not conceptualize the propositions defining the scenario (e.g., G2 in the Gettier case) as reasons or evidence. This difference comes out clearly in the pair of target questions given above:

(A) We consider the Gettier scenario and consider the question of whether Smith is justified in believing that either Jones owns a Ford or Brown is in Barcelona.

(B) We consider the Gettier scenario and consider the question of whether Smith and Jones are friends, but not *very* close friends.

In the case of (A), we do not look for *evidence* (reasons) in G2 for Smith's being justified. Instead, we would look for an explanation of why Smith is justified; the fact that he is justified being settled intuitively. By contrast, in (B), we do look for evidence in G2; we try to find some indication of the relative closeness of Smith's and Jones's friendship.

In these first two subsections, I have argued that intuition is needed to account for inference, at least in cases where the resulting assertive attitudes are epistemically evaluable – and this is so even for relatively simple cases of inference Although these intuitions are essential for giving an account of the rationality of inferential judgment, they do not figure in a substantive way into the justificatory status of the resulting beliefs – which is largely determined by the justificatory status of the premise beliefs.

4.4 Perceptual Seemings, Presentational Content, & Intuition

The argument for the involvement of intuitions in inference turns on the pair of claims that concept application involves intuition and inference requires deploying the concept of reasons (among, possibly, others). If correct, this result goes a long way toward establishing the involvement of intuitions in the vast majority of our knowledge, including the vast majority of our empirical knowledge. At the same time, this way of defending the indispensability thesis is relatively thin in the sense that it invokes only a limited number of concepts (reasons, conclusion, epistemic support). And while that would not be a trivial result, it undersells the centrality of intuitions in the acquisition of empirical knowledge. In this final subsection, I will argue that intuition plays an indispensable role not only in the inferences we make from our perceptual experiences, but in a large number of those perceptual experiences themselves.

From the point of view of Presentationalism, the crucial question about perceptual seemings is: What are their *presentational* contents? That is, what states of affairs are presented by (ostensibly revealed by) our perceptual seemings? This way of framing the issue is designed to avoid as much as possible taking specific stands on the detailed mechanics of perceptual learning, and I believe philosophers should be extremely reluctant to do so. In particular, this discussion does not turn on the still unsettled debate over whether perception (the perceptual system) represents kinds as such (Burnston 2023) or the much-discussed "dividing line" between perception and cognition (e.g., Block 2023). At least part of the reason for this neutrality is that there is no consensus as to what constitutes the visual system in the first place. Braddick & Atkinson, for instance, note that "the more we know about the brain networks linking vision to decision, action, and recognition, the more we recognize the essential continuity of these processes, especially given the ubiquitous feedback loops that infuse information from 'higher' areas into early visual processing" (2020, 897).

The methodology here is to begin from a more secure starting point – consideration of the contents presented by perceptual experiences. This issue is more amenable to philosophical investigation because it is less subject to the vagaries of scientific theory development and less likely to turn on contingent features of the human perceptual apparatus. Presumably, for instance, perceptual experience is multiply realizable in ways that shift any hypothesized way of drawing the perception/cognition distinction from where it is located in our own case. So, there is not any presumption that perceptual seemings correspond to the output of a hypothesized visual system. That may be so, and, if it is so, then defenders of higher-order perceptual contents may be vindicated. But this result is inessential to the argument or to my ultimate proposal. What is essential is that they are presentational states, not that they are visual states or purely visual states. Presentationalism should not be concerned with such distinctions *except* insofar as they potentially impact the potential for presentational states to serve as foundational justifiers (as I will discuss below). So, Presentationalism is not wholly neutral on the results of scientific investigation, but it is arguably independent of many of the details of implementation that are often bandied about in the philosophy of perception.[60]

At face value, the answer to the question of what the presentational contents of perceptual experiences are is that they present a robust, four-dimensional world of external objects of specific kinds. Strawson captures this point nicely:

> Suppose [we ask] a non-philosophical observer [to give a description of their current visual experience] ... [They] might reply in some such terms as these: "I see the red light of the setting sun filtering through the black and thickly clustered branches of the elms; I see the dappled deer grazing in groups on the vivid green grass ... " and so on. So, we ... explain that we want him to amend his account so that, without any sacrifice of fidelity to the experience as actually enjoyed, it nevertheless sheds all that heavy load of commitment to propositions about the world .... Our observer ... does not start talking about lights and colours, patches and patterns. For he sees that to do so would be to falsify the character of the experience .... He says, instead, ... "[T]he simplest way to do this ... is to ... describe my visual experience [thus]: "I had a visual experience such as it would have been natural to describe by saying that I saw, etc. ... " (1979, 43–44).

Strawson's non-philosophical observer astutely observes here that the presentational content of perceptual experience can only be accurately captured if we make use of certain "high-level" properties such as deer, elm, sun, grass, etc. This characterization is not unique to Strawson. Other representative examples include:

- [S]eeing seems to "bring one into direct contact with remote objects" and to reveal their shapes and colours. (Broad 1952, 6)
- Visual phenomenology makes it for a subject as if a scene is simply presented. (Sturgeon 2000, 9)
- [M]y perceptual experience seems to directly present physical objects and situations to me (Bonjour 2004, 354).
- The ripe tomato seems immediately present to me in experience. (Levine 2006, 179).

Moreover, as Strawson goes on to observe, leaving out these higher-order features in favor of only "lower-level" properties would "falsify the character of the experience".

Consider Firth's round-up of philosophical attempts to characterize the sense-data purportedly presented by visual perception:

---

[60] This will be particularly true if one accepts (as I do) an even moderate degree of Quinean underdetermination (Quine 1951, 1960).

> With respect to visual perception, for example, [sense-data theorists] agree with Berkeley that it is false to say that 'we immediately perceive by sight anything beside light, and colours, and figures'. Thus, our sense-datum when we look at a dog, according to Russell, is 'a canoid patch of colour'. And when we look at a penny stamp, according to Broad, our sensum is 'a red patch of approximately square shape'. And when we look at an apple, according to Lewis, what is given is a 'round, ruddy ... somewhat'. And when we look at a tomato, according to Price, our sense-datum is 'a red patch of a round and somewhat bulgy shape'." (Firth 1949, 438).

The tortured nature of these descriptions is evident. When we look at a dog, what is *presented* to us is decidedly not a dog-shaped patch of color, but a dog.[61]

Here, in outline, is the argument based on Strawson's observation:

1. Ordinary perceptual reports have presentational contents that invoke higher-level concepts.
2. All rephrasals of the presentational contents of those reports omitting reference to higher-level concepts are inaccurate (i.e., they "falsify their character").
3. Therefore, higher-level concepts are essential to accurately specifying the presentational contents of perceptual reports.

On the assumption that perceptual reports of this sort capture what we take the presentational content of perceptual seemings to be, Strawson's argument suggests that perceptual seemings involve higher-order presentational content.

This assessment of presentational contents is supported by an additional consideration that is central to Presentationalism. As we have seen, one of the main functional characteristics of presentational states is that they tend to generate overridable inclinations to believe their contents. So, one way of determining the presentational content of perceptual experiences is by considering which doxastic inclinations those experiences give rise to and which they do not. In this regard, consider, for example, the case of color constancies (Noë 2005). I am sitting at my desk looking at a uniformly off-white colored wall. Toward the ceiling, the smoke detector casts a shadow, creating a darker patch. My inclination is to judge that there is a uniformly off-white colored wall with a shadow cast on it. With some effort, I can conceptually understand a visual field involving color variance. But it does not seem like anything is *presented* to me as varying in color, and I certainly have no inclination to judge that the wall (or anything else I see) varies in color.

---

[61] See McNeill (2016) for an argument against the Surface View – the view that we see objects in virtue of seeing their facing surfaces. Related points can be found in Peacocke (1983) and Smith (2000).

There are two considerations at play. First, perceptual seemings naturally give rise to doxastic inclinations whose contents involve higher-level concepts. This first observation provides partial support for the claim that the presentational contents of perceptual seemings routinely involve higher-level concepts. However, MD ought to allow for the immediate justification of beliefs whose content differs from the presentational content of seemings. For instance, we may be immediately justified in judging certain simple logical entailments of the presentational contents of our seemings rather than those contents themselves. And, for this reason, it is not decisive. Nevertheless, taken in conjunction with Strawson's argument, it provides us with some confirmation for higher-level presentational content in perception.

The second consideration is that perceptual experiences don't typically give rise to doxastic inclinations that invoke only lower-level concepts. But intuitively, we should have such inclinations if perceptual seemings typically had purely lower-level presentational content. This consideration provides additional support for the second premise of Strawson's argument.

So, the presentational contents of perceptual seemings involve higher-level properties and not (at least not typically) purely lower-level properties. However, it doesn't follow from this that there are *phenomenological* differences between perceptual seemings differing in the specificity of their higher-order presentational contents. Lyons, for instance, offers the following example:

> *Copperhead:* Walking through a field, you and I come across a copperhead. I am a professional herpetologist, and it looks like a copperhead to me, though only like a snake to you (it also, of course, looks like a snake to me). Nonetheless, you and I have [phenomenologically] identical visual experiences (2005, 243).

Intuitively, the novice and the expert in *Copperhead* needn't differ phenomenologically in order for their perceptual experiences to present different states. All that is required is that things *seem* different to the novice and the expert. Reiland, following orthodoxy, maintains that such seemings "have a proprietary, quasi-sensory, and quasi-cognitive phenomenology in involving passive employment of conceptual capacities and representing something as being some way" (2014, 181). As Reiland notes, such seemings appear to involve the deployment of concepts (i.e., concept application). It is plausible, therefore, that the kind of seeming involved in generating higher-level presentational content in perceptual experience is an intuition. Roughly, perceptual experience is a complex seeming composed of a basic perceptual seeming and a compresent intuition.[62] This neo-Kantian view

---

[62] Reiland distinguishes three components to perceptual experience: (1) sensations, (2) perceptual experiences, and (3) seemings. "On this view, seemings are interface states which mediate

treats the combination of basic perceptual seemings (apperceptive seemings) and concept-application intuitions as generating the robust higher-level presentational content we routinely experience in perception/perceptual experience.

However, since I have already argued that intuitions lack any (or any substantive) phenomenology, there is no reason to think that the novice and the expert are in substantively different phenomenological states. This result accounts for the dialectical stalemate over phenomenal contrast arguments (Bayne 2009, Siegel 2006). Reminiscent of the Absent Intuition Challenge, if non-phenomenological (or weakly phenomenological) seemings account for the presence of higher-level concepts in perceptual experience, there will be little to no clear phenomenological difference between experts and novices and, consequently, the introspective results of our judgements are likely to be "regimented by the view initially held" (Furst 2017).[63]

This view also provides an independently motivated response to McGrath's (2017) influential Only-Because Argument against (Liberal) Presentationalism. According to McGrath, our expert's knowledge above that it is a copperhead epistemically presupposes knowledge of what copperheads look like. If so, then the expert's resulting belief that is a copperhead is not immediate. Here, more explicitly, is the argument:

The Only-Because Argument

1. S knows that those are Fs, and S knows what Fs look like.
2. If S has an epistemizer for *those are Fs* that don't include her knowledge of what Fs look like, then if S didn't know what Fs look like, she would still be in a position to know that those are Fs.
3. However, if S didn't know what Fs look like, S wouldn't be in a position to know that those are Fs.
4. Every epistemizer S has for those are Fs includes her knowledge of what Fs look like. (From 2 and 3).

---

between sensation/perception on the one hand and central cognition on the other by putting sensory or perceptual data into a conceptual format usable by the cognitive system" (2015, 512). I am using "perceptual experiences" in a way that I think corresponds more closely to ordinary language (as, for example, in perception reports) to indicate the final output state that is fed into the cognitive system. State (2) might be thought of as what cognitive neuroscientists dub the apperceptive stage. "At the level of form perception, [Lissauer] proposed that visual recognition required processing through two distinct stages: the first (apperception) he described as "the stage of conscious awareness of a sensory impression"; the second (or associative stage) was believed to result from the simultaneous activation of many concepts related to the object (i.e., the activation of associated memories)" (Riddoch & Humphreys 2003, 501). Similar views can be found in (Brogaard, 2013, 2014; Lyons, 2005, 2009; Tucker, 2010).

[63] Other recent criticisms along these lines include (Fulkerson & Cohen, 2025; Jorba & Vicente, 2020; Koksvik 2015).

5. Knowledge of what Fs look like is propositional knowledge.
6. Therefore, S's knowledge that those are Fs is mediated knowledge. (From 1, 4, and 5).[64]

There is a fair amount to be concerned with in this argument from the point of view of Presentationalism. The Presentationalist is only committed to the claim that it seems to S that those are Fs. While it is plausible that such seemings presuppose some additional recognitional capacity, it is not obvious that S has to *know what* Fs look like in order for it to seem to S that those are Fs. However, McGrath's discussion assumes that S must know what Fs look like and then focuses on possible interpretations of knowledge-what. This has the effect of loading the discussion in ways that allow him to press his conclusion by comparison to the intellectualism/anti-intellectualism debate over knowledge-how.

But the correct account of knowledge-*wh* and the correct background states necessary for higher-level presentational content are independent issues. To begin with, consider a knowledge-what version of Bengson & Moffett's (2011) account of knowledge-how:

> The relation of knowledge what Fs look like is a (non-propositional, non-behavioral-dispositional) *objectual* attitude to a way Fs look.

McGrath considers and correctly rejects objectualist or anti-intellectualist theories of knowledge what Fs look like. But this does not settle the issue. The proposal made by Bengson & Moffett, as well as others in the contemporary debate concerning knowledge-how, is concerned with knowledge-how *to*, that is, knowledge-how claims with finite complement clauses. The analogous knowledge of what claim would be knowledge of what to look for (in identifying Fs), not knowledge of what Fs look like.[65] The latter reports are more similar to knowledge-how *one* reports, which are widely accepted to have a propositionalist analysis. And surely knowing what to look for (in identifying Fs) is as much an epistemizer for *those are Fs* as knowing what Fs look like. So, the correct objectualist analysis should be the following:

> *Objectualist Analysis*: The relation of knowledge what to look for in identifying Fs is a (non-propositional, non-behavioral-dispositional) *objectual* attitude toward the features to look for to identify Fs.

---

[64] This formulation is taken from Feeney (2020, 88).
[65] Or, more directly, knowledge of how to identify Fs, which seems to be an equally good epistemizer. But for the sake of dialectical uniformity, I will stick with the knowledge of what attributions.

What it is for S to know what to look for in identifying Fs is for S to know the features to look for in identifying Fs, so characterized.[66]

Now consider the expert in *Copperhead*. Let us grant that she knows what copperheads look like. Still, it is also plausible that she knows what to look for (i.e., such-and-such markings) to identify copperheads.[67] Knowing what to look for is a variety of knowing what to φ.[68] Considerations similar to those adduced by Bengson & Moffett (Bengson & Moffett 2011, 182–185) against an intellectualist theory of knowledge appear to equally favor an objectualist analysis of knowing what-to attributions. For instance, consider the following:

a. Sara knows what to look for better than Miguel.
b. # Sara knows that F is the relevant feature better than Miguel.
c. Sara knows the features to look for better than Miguel.

Or again:

d. Sara knows that Ψ are the relevant features – in fact, she's certain of it.
e. # Sara knows what to look for – in fact, she is certain of it.
f. Sara knows what to look for – in fact, she is an expert at it.
g. Sara knows the features to look for – in fact, she is an expert at it.

The same pattern holds for the other features of knowledge that were identified by Bengson & Moffett.

At the same time, knowing what to look for in identifying Fs is not merely an ability or disposition. Our expert herpetologist will still know what to look for even if she has recently lost her sight (cf. Stanley & Williamson's 2001 pianist example, 416). While such simple examples do not settle the case, the rest of the debate appears to play out along familiar lines. But in the case of knowing-what-to, the intuitive case is considerably stronger than in the case of knowing-how-

---

[66] McGrath objects to his target version of objectualism that "Merely knowing a way of looking that is in fact the way [Fs] look isn't enough" to know that those are Fs (2017, 19). It seems that McGrath assumes that these ascriptions aren't fine-grained enough to capture the relevant knowledge. For instance, in discussing the claim that knowing a way Fs look is not sufficient to know that those are Fs he asks: "Why can't [S] know the way of looking to the last detail, and be able to recognize it again on sight, but still not associate it with the category F?" (19). But the intention is that the attitude is toward a way Fs look, *so characterized or qua Fs* (Forbes 2000). So, for instance, our expert on *Copperhead* knows the way copperheads (*qua* copperheads) look. The novice may, in fact, know the way copperheads look, but not *qua* copperheads. The same point about the intensionality of objectual attitudes holds for the alternative objectualist analysis proposed here.

[67] A triangular head, copper-to-tan color with a diagnostic hourglass pattern on a stocky body.

[68] Other instances include knowing what to do (in case of fire), knowing what to say (in times of crisis), and knowing what to move (in a game of chess). Knowing what to φ is, in turn, a variety of knowledge-wh to φ, which includes knowing where to φ, knowing why to φ, knowing when to φ, and (possibly) knowing whether to φ. A recent discussion may be found in Jerzak & Kocurek (2025). Though I am skeptical of their conclusions, I do not have the space to address them here.

to. As any novice birder can attest, knowing what to look for in identifying bird species does not ensure any ability or disposition to identify them.

Feeney (2020), in objecting along similar lines to the Only-Because Argument, adopts a non-doxastic epistemizer for those who are Fs in terms of recognitional dispositions.

Recognitional Competence: S has a competence to recognize Fs *iff*:

(1) There is a property of Fs, G-ness, such that S is disposed to believe [aptly] that x is F (absent defeaters) if she perceives that x is G (under relevant conditions).

(2) For any property H-ness that is not a looks property of Fs, it's not the case that S is disposed to believe that x is F if she perceives that x is H (all other things being equal).

While recognitional competence, so understood, is surely a feature of *expert* perception, it cannot do the work required here. First, as far as the question of higher-level presentational content goes, recognitional *competence* is not required; incompetence will serve quite as well. Assuming expert perception is a form of perceptual learning, it seems obvious that we can also learn incorrectly. Second, this dispositional approach suffers from the same complaint I levelled against Williamson's account of the Gettier cases – it leaves us with brute doxastic inclinations to believe propositions with higher-level content without providing an account of any pre-doxastic seeming state that rationalizes those inclinations. But, as we saw in the discussion of Strawson's argument, our perceptual experiences themselves seem to have such content, and Feeney's proposal does not account for this. To avoid this problem, Feeney needs to provide some account of the non-aberrancy of these doxastic inclinations as well as the *prima facie* reasonableness (both from the first-person and third-person perspective) of giving in to those inclinations.

The theory of intuitionally enhanced perceptual experiences fills this lacuna. Indeed, the proposed kind of knowledge – knowledge of what to look for – is naturally understood as fleshing out Feeney's general idea in two ways. The first is to modify Feeney's theory of recognitional competence with a theory of attentional weighting of the sort proposed by Ransom (2020). Roughly:

Categorial Recognition: S perceptually categorizes Fs by way of a (complex) property G *iff*

(1) S is disposed to shift her attention to G in apperceptive presentations (under relevant conditions), and

(2) In virtue of (1), it thereby (conceptually) seems to S that some component of her experience is an F. (That is, S thereby has the intuition that something is F.)

This proposal allows for our perceptual recognition to be in error when the features we "look for" in attentional weighting are erroneously taken to isolate Fs.

While this theory of intuitionally enhanced perception could be fleshed out in various ways, the basic outline is plausible: Higher-level presentational contents involved in normal perceptual experience arise from concept-application intuitions (presentations) generated by low-level visual presentational states. If so, higher-level presentational contents do not threaten the epistemic basicness of perceptual experiences since perceptual experiences are (in the sense proposed in Chudnoff 2011) *constituted* by all and only presentational states.

4.5 Conclusion

It is possible to read Descartes's *Meditations* as opening with a rationalist gambit: (1) first, to argue that even the totality of our perceptual evidence, in isolation, is unable by itself to secure an adequate foundation for any of our knowledge claims, and (2) to show that there is another source of evidence ("clear and distinct perception") which, when included as a distinct, sui generis source of evidence, allows us to recover all or most of what we prephilosophically thought we knew. Descartes's argument, thus, aims to show not only that eschewing intuition will leave us unable to capture recherché *a priori* knowledge but even basic empirical knowledge, particularly our knowledge of the external world. This argumentative strategy is an extremely attractive one for defenders of intuition. After all, defenders of intuitions do not merely claim that intuition is a convenient add-on to intellectual inquiry, but an indispensable element of such inquiry.

In this Element, I have argued that this is exactly what we find. Intuitions do not function as isolated evidential modalities directly relevant only to circumscribed classes of belief. Instead, they are integrated into virtually every component of our epistemic functioning. The strategy has been to argue that intuitions play a role, not just in establishing general foundational principles that are essential to knowledge (e.g., the axioms of logic and mathematics), but an ongoing and ubiquitous role in our everyday cognitive functioning. It is in this sense that I have argued for the indispensability of intuitions.

References

Aleci, C., & Dutto, K. 2024. Seeing the invisible: Theory and evidence of blindsight. *Discover Medicine*, **1**: 1–22.

Andrews, K. 2020. *The Animal Mind* (2nd Ed.). New York: Routledge.

Anscombe, G. E. M. 1957. *Intention*. Oxford: Blackwell.

1981. On sensations of position, in *Collected Philosophical Papers*, vol. 2: *Metaphysics and the Philosophy of Mind*: New York: Blackwell.

Arruda, C., & Povinelli, D. 2018. Two ways of relating to (and acting for) reasons. *Mind & Language*, **33**: 441–459.

Båve, A. 2017. Self-consciousness and reductive functionalism. *The Philosophical Quarterly*, **67**: 1–21.

Bayne, T. 2009. Perception and the reach of phenomenal content. *Philosophical Quarterly*, **59**: 385–404.

Bealer, G. 1987. The philosophical limits of scientific essentialism. *Philosophical Perspectives*, **1**: 289–365.

1992. The incoherence of empiricism. *Proceedings of the Aristotelian Society, Supplementary Volume*, **66**: 99–138.

1993b. Universals. *The Journal of Philosophy*, **90**: 5–32.

1996a. On the possibility of philosophical knowledge. *Philosophical Perspectives*, **10**: 1–34.

1996b. A priori knowledge and the scope of philosophy. *Philosophical Studies*, **81**: 121–142.

1997. Self-consciousness. *The Philosophical Review*, **106**: 69–117.

1998a. A theory of concepts and concept possession. *Philosophical Issues: Concepts*, **9**: 261–301.

1998b. Intuition and the autonomy of philosophy. In M. R. DePaul & W. Ramsey (eds.), *Rethinking Intuition*, 201–239. Lanham, Md.: Rowman and Littlefield.

2000. Fregean equivocation and ramsification on sparse theories: Response to McCullagh. *Mind & language*, **15**(5): 500–510.

2001. The self-consciousness argument: Why Tooley's criticisms fail. *Philosophical Studies*, **105**: 281–307.

2010. The Self-consciousness argument: Functionalism and the corruption of content. In Koons and Bealer (eds.), *The Waning of Materialism*, 137–158. New York: Oxford.

Beck, J. 2012. Do animals engage in conceptual thought? *Philosophy Compass*, **7**: 218–229.

Bengson, J. 2013. Experimental attacks on intuitions and answers. *Philosophy and Phenomenological Research* **86**: 495–532.

2015a. The intellectual given. *Mind*, **124**: 708–760.

2024. Intuition in philosophical inquiry. In McCain, Stapleford, & Steup (Eds.), *Seemings: New Arguments, New Angles*, 162–183. New York: Routledge.

2015b. Grasping the third realm. *Oxford Studies in Epistemology*, **5**: 1–38.

2020. The myth of quick and easy intuitions. In Biggs & Giersson (eds.), *The Routledge Handbook of Linguistic Reference*, 560–576. New York: Routledge.

Bengson, J., & Moffett, M. A. 2011. Nonpropositional intellectualism. In Bengson & Moffett (eds.), *Knowing How*, 161–195. New York: Oxford.

Berger J. 2020. Perceptual consciousness plays no epistemic role. *Philosophical Issues*, **30**: 7–23.

Berger J., Nanay B., & Quilty-Dunn J. 2018. Unconscious perceptual justification. *Inquiry*, **61**: 569–589.

Bergmann, M. 2006. *Justification without Awareness*. New York: Oxford University Press.

Block, N. 2007. Consciousness, accessibility and the mesh between psychology and neuroscience, *Behavioral and Brain Sciences*, **30**: 481–548.

1995. On a confusion about a function of consciousness. *Behavioral and Brain Sciences*, **18**: 227–247.

1980. Troubles with functionalism. In Block (ed.), *Readings in the Philosophy of Psychology*, 268–305. Vol. 1. Cambridge, MA: Harvard.

2023. *The Border between Seeing and Thinking*. New York: Oxford.

Boghossian, P. 2001. Inference and insight. *Philosophy and Phenomenological Research*, **63**: 633–640.

2014. What is inference? *Philosophical Studies*, **169**: 1–18.

2015. Is (determinate) meaning a naturalistic phenomenon. In S. Gross, N. Tebben, & M. Williams (eds.), *Meaning without Representation*, 331–358. New York: Oxford.

2019. Inference, agency, and responsibility. In M. Balcerak-Jackson & B. Balcerak-Jackson (eds.), *Reasoning*. New York: Oxford.

2020a. Intuition, understanding, and the a priori. Chapter 13 in Boghossian and Williamson, *Debating the a Priori*. New York: Oxford.

2020b. Reply to Williamson on intuition, understanding, and the a priori. Chapter 15 in Boghossian and Williamson, *Debating the a Priori*. New York: Oxford.

BonJour, L. 1980. Externalist theories of empirical knowledge. *Midwest Studies in Philosophy*, **5**: 53–74.

2004. In search of direct realism. *Philosophy and Phenomenological Research*, **69**: 349–367.

Borg, E., Harrison, R., Stazicker, J., & Salomons, T. 2020. Is the folk concept of pain polyeidic? *Mind & Language*, **35**: 29–47.

Braddick, O., & Atkinson, J. 2020. Review of Connolly, K. *Perceptual Learning. Perception*, **49**: 897–899.

Broad, C. D. 1952. Some elementary reflexions on sense-perception. *Philosophy*, **27**: 3–17.

Brogaard, B. 2015. Perceptual report. In M. Matthen (ed.), *The Oxford Handbook of the Philosophy of Perception*, 237–253. New York: Oxford.

2013. Phenomenal seemings and sensible dogmatism. In C. Tucker (ed.), *Seemings and Justification*, 270–289. New York: Oxford.

2014. Seeing as a non-experiential mental state: The case from synesthesia and visual imagery. In R. Brown (ed.), *Consciousness inside and out*, 377–394. Dordrecht: Springer.

Broome, J. 2013. *Rationality through Reasoning*. Malden, MA: Wiley-Blackwell.

Burge, T. 1979. Individualism and the Mental. *Midwest Studies in Philosophy*, **4**:73–121.

Burnston, D. C. 2023. How to think about higher-level perceptual contents. *Mind & Language*, **38**: 1166–1186.

Camp, E. 2017. Perspectives in imaginative engagement with fiction. *Philosophical Perspectives*, **31**: 73–102.

Celesia, G. G. 2005. Visual perception and awareness. *Journal of Psychophysiology*, **24**: 62–67.

Chalmers, D. 1997. *The Conscious Mind*. New York: Oxford.

Chudnoff, E. 2013. *Intuition*. New York: Oxford.

2024. Inferential seemings. In U. Kriegel (ed.), *Oxford Studies in the Philosophy of Mind*, 311–333. *Vol. 4*. New York: Oxford.

2020. *Forming Impressions*. New York: Oxford.

2011. What intuitions are like. *Philosophy and Phenomenological Research*, **82**: 625–654.

Cohen, S. 1984. Justification and truth. *Philosophical Studies*, **46**: 279–295.

Devitt, M. 2006. Intuitions in linguistics. *British Journal for the Philosophy of Science*, **57**: 481–513.

Dokic, J., & Martin, J.-R. 2017. Felt reality and the opacity of perception. *Topoi*, **36**: 299–309.

Feeney, M. 2020. Recognitional competence and knowing what things look like. *Philosophical Issues*, **30**: 86–101.

Ferretti, G. 2025. Philosophical implications of derealization disorder. *Synthese*, **205**, 1. https://doi.org/10.1007/s11229-024-04808-4.

Firth, R. 1949. Sense-data and the percept theory. *Mind*, **58**: 434–465.

Flanagan, O., & Polger, T. 1995. Zombies and the function of consciousness. *Journal of Consciousness Studies*, **2**: 313–321.

Fodor, J. A. 1974. Special sciences (Or: The disunity of science as a working hypothesis). *Synthese*, **28**: 97–115.

Forbes, G. 2000. Objectual attitudes. *Linguistics and Philosophy*, **23**: 141–183.

Foster, J. 2000. *The Nature of Perception*. New York: Oxford.

Friedman, J. 2019. Inquiry and belief. *Noûs*, **53**: 296–315.

Fulkerson, M., & Cohen, J. 2025. A new obstacle for phenomenal contrast. *The Philosophical Quarterly*, https://doi.org/10.1093/pq/pqaf009.

Funkhouser, E. 2023. Determinate/determinable. In A. R. J. Fisher & Anna-Sofia Maurin, *The Routledge Handbook of Properties*, 115–124. New York: Routledge.

Fürst, M. 2017. On the limits of the method of phenomenal contrast. *Journal of the American Philosophical Association*, **3**: 168–188.

Gertler, B. 2007. 2011. *Self-knowledge*. New York: Routledge.

Ghijsen, H. 2014. Phenomenalist dogmatist experientialism and the distinctiveness problem. *Synthese*, **191**(7): 1549–1566.

Gopnik, A., & Schwitzgebel, E. 1998. Whose concepts are they, anyway? The role of philosophical intuition in empirical psychology. In M. R. De Paul & W. Ramsey (eds.), *Rethinking Intuition*, 75–91. Lanham, MD: Rowan & Littlefield.

Hetherington, S. 2011. How to know: A practicalist conception of knowledge. Malden, MA: Wiley-Blackwell.

Huemer, M. 2007. Compassionate phenomenal conservatism. *Philosophy and Phenomenological Research*, **74**: 30–55.

2016. Inferential appearances. In B. Coppenger & M. Bergmann (eds.), *Intellectual Assurance*, 144–160. New York: Oxford.

2001. *Skepticism and the Veil of Perception*. Rowman & Littlefield.

Jenkin, Z. 2020. The epistemic role of core cognition. *Philosophical Review*, **129**: 251–298.

Jerzak, E., & Kocurek, A. W. 2025. Knowing what to do. *Noûs*, **59**: 160–190.

Johnston, M. 2007. Objective mind and the objectivity of our minds. *Philosophy and Phenomenological Research*, **75**: 233–268.

Jones, D. M. 2017. *The Biological Foundations of Action*. New York: Routledge.

Jorba, M., & Vicente, A. 2020. Phenomenal contrast arguments: What they achieve. *Mind & Language*, **35**: 350–367.

Koksvik, O. 2021. *Intuition as Conscious Experience*. New York: Routledge.

2015. Phenomenal contrast: A critique. *American Philosophical Quarterly*, **52**: 321–334.

2017. The phenomenology of intuition. *Philosophy Compass*, **12**: e12387, https://doi.org/10.1111/phc3.12387.

Kornblith, H. 1998. The role of intuition in philosophical inquiry: An account with no unnatural ingredients. In M. R. DePaul & W. Ramsey (eds.) *Rethinking Intuition*, 129–141. Lanham, Md: Rowan and Littlefield.

Kriegel, U. 2015. How to speak of existence: A Brentanian approach to (linguistic and mental) ontological commitment. *Grazer Philosophische Studien*, **91**: 81–106.

Levine, J. 2006. Conscious awareness and (self-) representation. In U. Kriegel & K. Williford (eds.), *Self-Representational Approaches to Consciousness*, 173–198. Cambridge, MA: MIT

Levy, N. 2014. *Consciousness & Moral Responsibility*. New York: Oxford.

Lewis, D. 1970. How to define theoretical terms. *Journal of Philosophy*, **67**: 427–446.

1983. Postscript to 'Mad pain and Martian pain'. Philosophical Papers, Vol. 1. New York: Oxford.

Liu, M. 2023. The polysemy view of pain. *Mind & Language*, **38**: 198–217.

Ludwig, K. 2007. The epistemology of thought experiments: First person versus third person approaches. *Midwest Studies in Philosophy*, **31**: 128–159.

2010. Intuitions and relativity. *Philosophical Psychology*, **23**: 427–445.

2018. Thought experiments and experimental philosophy. In M. T. Stuart, Y. Fehige, & J. R. Brown (eds.), *The Routledge Companion to Thought Experiments*, 385–405. New York: Routledge.

Lyons, J. 2005. Perceptual belief and nonexperiential looks. *Philosophical Perspectives*, **19**: 237–256.

2009. *Perception and Basic Beliefs*. New York: Oxford.

Ludwig, K. 2007. The epistemology of thought experiments: First person versus third person approaches. Midwest Studies in Philosophy, XXXI, 129–159

Machery, E. 2017. *Philosophy within Its Proper Bounds*. New York: Oxford.

Malmgren, A. S. 2018. Varieties of inference?. *Philosophical Issues*, **28**: 221–254.

McCain, K., & Moretti, L. 2021. *Appearance and Explanation*. New York: Oxford.

McCain, K., & Stapleford, S. 2024. Appearances and the Problem of Stored Beliefs. In K. McCain, S. Stapleford, & M. Steup (eds.), *Seemings: New Arguments, New Angles*, 63–74. New York: Routledge.

McCullagh, M. 2000. Functionalism and self-consciousness. *Mind & Language*, **15**: 481–499.

McGrath, M. 2017. Knowing what things look like. *Philosophical Review*, **126**: 1–41.

Mcneill, W. 2016. The visual role of objects' facing surfaces. *Philosophy and Phenomenological Research*, **92**: 411–431.

Meinong, A. 1983 (1903). *On Assumptions*, 2nd ed. James Heanue (trans.). Berkeley, CA: University of California Press.

Miyazono, K. 2021. Visual experiences without presentational phenomenology. *Ergo*, **8**: 551–576. https://doi.org/10.3998/ergo.1156.

Moffett, M. 2010. Against a posteriori functionalism. *Canadian Journal of Philosophy*, **40**: 83–106.

2025. Basic epistemic reasons: An action-theoretic proposal. *Ratio*, **38**: 93–101.

2023. Intuitions as evidence: An introduction. In M. Lasonen-Aarnio & C. Littlejohn (Eds.), *The Routledge Handbook of the Philosophy of Evidence*, 275–291. New York: Routledge.

2003. Knowing facts and believing propositions: A solution to the problem of doxastic shift. *Philosophical Studies*, **115**: 81–97.

Moon, A. 2012. Knowing without evidence. *Mind*, **121**: 309–331.

Moore, G. E. 1903. The refutation of Idealism. *Mind*, **12**: 433–453.

Myers, J. 2024. Imaginative beliefs. *Inquiry*, 1–28, doi: 10.1080/0020174X.2024.2312218.

Noë, A. 2005. Real presence. *Philosophical Topics*, **33**: 235–264.

Oppenheim, P., & Putnam, H. 1958. *Unity of science as a working hypothesis*. In Fiegl, Scriven, & Maxwell (eds.), Concepts, Theories and the Mind-Body Problem, Vol. 2. University of Minnesota Press.

Overgaard, M. 2012. Blindsight: Recent and historical controversies on the blindness of blindsight. *Wiley Interdisciplinary Reviews: Cognitive Science*, **3(6)**: 607–614.

Phillips, I. 2021. Blindsight is qualitatively degraded conscious vision. *Psychological Review*, **128**(3): 558.

Peacocke, C. 1983. *Sense and Content*. New York: Oxford.

Pryor, J. 2000. The skeptic and the dogmatist. *Noûs*, **34**: 517–549.

2005. There is immediate justification. In M. Steup, J. Turri & E. Sosa (eds.), *Contemporary Debates in Epistemology*, 202–243. New York: Blackwell.

Pust, J. 2000. *Intuitions as Evidence*. New York: Routledge.

Quine, W. V. O. 1951. Two dogmas of empiricism. *The Philosophical Review*, **60**: 20–43.

1960. *Word and Object*. Cambridge MA: MIT Press.

Ramsey, F. P. 1990 (1929). Theories. In D. H. Mellor (ed.), *Philosophical Papers*, 112–136. New York: Cambridge.

Ransom, M. 2020. Attentional weighting in perceptual learning. *Journal of Consciousness Studies*, **27**: 236–248.

Reiland, I. 2015. Experience, seemings, and evidence. *Pacific Philosophical Quarterly*, **96**: 510–534.

2014. On experiencing high level properties. *American Philosophical Quarterly*, **51**: 177–187.

Riccardi, M. 2019. *Synthese*, **196**: 2907–2926.

Richard, M. 2019. Is Reasoning a Form of Agency? In M. Balcerak-Jackson and B. Balcerak-Jackson (eds.), *Reasoning: Essays on Theoretical and Practical Thinking*, 91–100, New York: Oxford.

Riddoch, M. J., & Humphreys, G. W. 2003. Visual agnosia. *Neurologic Clinics*, **21**: 501–520.

Robertson, K., & Wilson, A. 2024. *Levels of Explanation*. New York: Oxford.

Schroeder, M. 2021. *Reasons First*. New York: Oxford.

Searle, J. 1983. *Intentionality*. New York: Cambridge University Press.

Shoemaker, S. 2001. Realization and mental causation. In C. Gillett & B. Loewer (eds.), *Physicalism and its Discontents*, 74–98. New York: Cambridge.

Shorvon J. H., Hill, J. D. N., Burkitt, E., & Halstead, H. 1946. The depersonalization syndrome. *Proceedings of the Royal Society of Medicine*, **39**: 779–792.

Siegel, S. 2019. Inference without reckoning. In M. Balcerak-Jackson & B. Balcerak-Jackson (eds.), *Reasoning: New Essays on Theoretical and Practical Thinking*, 15–31. New York: Oxford.

2017. *The Rationality of Perception*. New York: Oxford.

2006. Which properties are represented in perception? In T. Szabô Gendler and J. Hawthorne (eds.), *Perceptual Experience*, 481–503. New York: Oxford.

Smith, A. D. 2000. *The Problem of Perception*. Cambridge, MA: Harvard.

Smithies, D. 2012. The mental lives of zombies. *Philosophical Perspectives*, **26**: 343–372.

2013. The nature of cognitive phenomenology. *Philosophy Compass*, **8**: 744–754.

2014. The phenomenal basis of epistemic justification. In M. Sprevak & J. Kallestrup (eds.), *New Waves in Philosophy of Mind*, 98–124. London: Palgrave Macmillan.

2019. *The Epistemic Role of Consciousness*. New York: Oxford.

2021. Precis of *The Epistemic Role of Consciousness*. *Analysis Reviews*, **81**: 772–774.

2024. Inference without the taking condition. In K. McCain, S. Stapleford, & M. Steup (eds.), 130–146, *Seemings: New Arguments, New Angles*. New York: Routledge.

Sosa, E. 2006. Intuitions and truth. In P. Greenough & M. P. Lynch (eds.), *Truth and Realism*, 208–226. New York: Oxford.

1996. Rational intuition: Bealer on its nature and epistemic status. *Philosophical Studies*, **81**: 151–162.

Speaks, J. 2009. Transparency, intentionalism, and the nature of perceptual content. *Philosophy and Phenomenological Research*, **79**: 539–573.

Stanley, J., & Williamson, T. 2001. Knowing how. *Journal of Philosophy*, **98**: 411–444.

Stout, G. F. 2013 (1896). *Analytic Psychology*, Vol. I. New York: Routledge.

Strawson, P. F. 1992. Comments of Bealer's 'The incoherence of empiricism'. *Proceedings of the Aristotelian Society*, Supplementary Volumes, **66**: 139–143.

1979. Perception and its objects. In G. F. Macdonald (ed.), *Perception and Identity: Essays Presented to A. J. Ayer with His Replies*, 41–60. Ithaca, NY: Cornell University Press.

Sturgeon, S. 2000. *Matters of Mind: Consciousness, Reason, and Nature*. New York: Routledge.

Sytsma, J. 2015. Review of *Intuition*, by Elijah Chudnoff. *Australasian Journal of Philosophy*, **93**: 610–613.

Taylor, S. A., & Coppenger, B. 2024. Inferential internalism defended. *Southwest Philosophy Review*, **40**: 195–206.

Teng, L. 2024. The epistemic insignificance of phenomenal force. *Philosophy and Phenomenological Research*, **109**: 55–76.

Textor, M. 2021. Acquaintance, presentation and judgement: From Brentano to Russell and back again. *Inquiry*, https://doi.org/10.1080/0020174X.2021.1899043.

Theiler, N., Roelofsen, F., & Aloni, M. 2017. What's wrong with believing whether. *Semantics and Linguistic Theory*, **27**: 248–265.

Tolhurst, W. 1998. Seemings. *American Philosophical Quarterly*, **35**: 293–302.

Tooley, M. 2001. Functional concepts, referentially opaque contexts, causal relations, and the definition of theoretical terms. *Philosophical Studies*, **105**: 251–279.

Tucker, C. 2013. Seemings and justification: An introduction. In C. Tucker (ed.), *Seemings and Justification*, 1–29. New York: Oxford.

2010. Why open-minded people should endorse dogmatism. *Philosophical Perspectives*, **24**: 529–545.

Weiskrantz L, Warrington E., Sanders M., & Marshall J. (1974). Visual capacity in the hemianopic field following a restricted occipital ablation. *Brain*, **97**: 709–728.

Williamson, T. 2004. Philosophical 'intuitions' and scepticism about judgement. *Dialectica*, **58**: 109–153.

2007. *The Philosophy of Philosophy*. New York: Blackwell.

2020a. Reply to Boghossian on intuition, understanding, and the a prior. Chapter 14 in Boghossian and Williamson, *Debating the A Priori*. New York: Oxford.

2020b. Boghossian on intuition and the a priori once again. Chapter 16 in Boghossian and Williamson, *Debating the a Priori*. New York: Oxford.

Wilson, J. 1999. How superduper does a physicalist supervenience need to be?. *The Philosophical Quarterly*, **49**(194), 33–52.

Wu, W. 2023. *Movements of the Mind*. New York: Oxford.

Xu, F. 1997. From Lot's wife to a pillar of salt: Evidence that *physical object* is a sortal concept. *Mind & Language*, **12**: 365–392.

Yablo, S. 1992. Mental causation. *The Philosophical Review*, **101**: 245–280.

Acknowledgements

I would like to thank John Bengson, Chad Carmichael, and Dan Korman for their extensive discussion of this material. Their feedback has been invaluable. Thanks are also due to the Epistemology series editor, Stephen Hetherington, for helping to navigate the various submission steps and providing sound advice on the manuscript. Scott Lucas proofread the entire manuscript and made excellent suggestions. Finally, many thanks to my wife, Monique Foster, who not only provided support during a stressful period but indulged me in countless hours of philosophical discussion that helped clarify and improve many of the ideas.

— for George —

Cambridge Elements

Epistemology

Stephen Hetherington
University of New South Wales, Sydney

Stephen Hetherington is Professor Emeritus of Philosophy at the University of New South Wales, Sydney. He is the author of numerous books, including *Knowledge and the Gettier Problem* (Cambridge University Press, 2016), and *What Is Epistemology?* (Polity, 2019), and is the editor of several others, including *Knowledge in Contemporary Epistemology* (with Markos Valaris: Bloomsbury, 2019), and *What the Ancients Offer to Contemporary Epistemology* (with Nicholas D. Smith: Routledge, 2020). He was the Editor-in-Chief of the Australasian Journal of Philosophy from 2013 until 2022.

About the Series

This Elements series seeks to cover all aspects of a rapidly evolving field, including emerging and evolving topics such as: fallibilism; knowing how; self-knowledge; knowledge of morality; knowledge and injustice; formal epistemology; knowledge and religion; scientific knowledge; collective epistemology; applied epistemology; virtue epistemology; wisdom. The series demonstrates the liveliness and diversity of the field, while also pointing to new areas of investigation.

Cambridge Elements

Epistemology

Elements in the Series

Stratified Virtue Epistemology: A Defence
J. Adam Carter

The Skeptic and the Veridicalist: On the Difference Between Knowing What There Is and Knowing What Things Are
Yuval Avnur

Transcendental Epistemology
Tony Cheng

Knowledge and God
Matthew A. Benton

Knowing What It Is Like
Yuri Cath

Disagreement
Diego E. Machuca

On Believing and Being Convinced
Paul Silva Jr

Knowledge-First Epistemology: A Defence
Mona Simion

Emotional Self-Knowledge: How Affective Skills Reveal Our Values, Goals, Cares and Concerns
Matt Stichter and Ellen Fridland

Deception and Self-Deception: A Unified Account
Vladimir Krstić

The Epistemology of Logic
Ben Martin

The Indispensability of Intuitions
Marc A. Moffett

A full series listing is available at: www.cambridge.org/EEPI

For EU product safety concerns, contact us at Calle de José Abascal, 56–1°, 28003 Madrid, Spain or eugpsr@cambridge.org.

www.ingramcontent.com/pod-product-compliance
Lightning Source LLC
LaVergne TN
LVHW011857060526
838200LV00054B/4387